Widowed
and
Moving Forward

Insights on Managing Grief, Dating & Blending Families

Widowed
and
Moving Forward

Insights on Managing Grief, Dating & Blending Families

Justin T. Eller & Jennifer M. Eller

R

"*Widowed and Moving Forward* provides a much-needed voice in the space of managing grief, dating, and blending families among LDS bereavement. It's written specifically for those who wish to navigate the uncertain path of moving forward after widowhood. Justin and Jennifer approach these difficult topics from personal experience and with compassion, practicality, and humor. Their stories frequently brought tears to my eyes both for the sorrows endured and the triumphs won. This thoughtful book will help the reader understand and honor the pain of those who grieve, recognize trauma, and realize hope in the healing love of our Savior, Jesus Christ. For anyone wishing to move into a relationship after losing a loved one, this is a must-read."

– Shauna Packer

National Award-Winning Author of *Destroying Their God: How I Fought My Evil Half-Brother to Save My Children*

"A wonderfully well-written book. The stories that Justin and Jennifer share make me fully understand that I am not alone in my grief and my remarriage journey. It's an excellent read and highly relatable. This book provides hope for anyone who is moving forward after the loss of a spouse."

– Lisa McClean

Blogger-Blended Hope
www.blendedhope.com

"I'm an adult child living in a blended family. *Widowed and Moving Forward* spoke to me in an amazing way. It is full of inspiration that anyone could find uplifting. There are sad parts, hopeful parts, joyful parts, and everything in between."

– Sienna Von Gunten

Daughter of a Surviving Parent

"It's not easy to find a book that covers so many sensitive topics in relation to being widowed, dating, and blending families. I can relate to many things that are illustrated in this book. I find it to be insightful and real. It helped me to build reasonable expectations for what can happen in the future after being widowed. I am thankful for the example shown in all the stories shared of real people with real families, ultimately blended with real love. I would recommend it to anyone who has experienced the loss of a spouse, and is wondering where to go from there."

– *Lara Stice Palmer*
Remarried Widow

"An intimate look at the issues facing surviving spouses bearing the unbearable in the landscape of loss. This book tackles universal themes that accompany bereavement, including the difficult issue of trauma. It also offers hope and insights for rebuilding, including creating new connections, deciding to love again, and blending families. Full of personal stories, this book serves as a guide to those who are facing a similar journey through unplanned and relatively uncharted territory."

– *Kristina Anderson*
Content Strategist & MPC

"In *Widowed and Moving Forward*, the authors take a practical and heartfelt approach in sharing their experiences. What makes it a unique experience is that they are both widowed. Finding new experiences to laugh about is crucial, while still cherishing memories and traditions of the past. They describe how to do this while sharing their experience in blending families together."

– *Russell J. Butler*
Creator of Good Grief

"*Widowed and Moving Forward* explores the roller coaster of emotions associated with grieving the death of a spouse while trying to be a source of strength for your children—only to face another major curve when remarrying and blending two unique families.

"What I admire about this story is they don't go it alone: they believe in Jesus Christ and, as a result, they're not defined by their last names or their blood. They are defined by a commitment of love."

– *Paul Cardall*
Dove Award-Winning Pianist

Editorial work by Eschler Editing
Cover design by Brian Halley
Photography by Jessica White Photography and Madison Pratt (www.mpfilmandphoto.com)
Interior print design and layout by Sydnee Hyer
Ebook design and layout by Sydnee Hyer
Production services facilitated by Scrivener Books

Published by Resilience

ISBN: 978-1-949165-24-1

In Loving Memory of Angela Sargent Eller
and Stoney Burke Winterton

Contents

Preface

When I began this project I anticipated writing solely about blending families. But I realized early on that mine and Jen's backgrounds in first being widowed, and then adult dating, has given our coming together a genuineness that couldn't be ignored. I began interviewing Jen about some of the experiences we've had both when we were apart and now that we are together. Her insight was so valuable that I've included much of it in this book. The message that she presents is powerful. I've also included entries from two of our children which adds perspective that a parent couldn't replicate.

None of our collective children had graduated high school at the time Jen and I each lost a spouse, and they lost a parent. As one might imagine, our children knew what it was like to do hard things before we'd ever met. It makes my heart hurt to think about. Now that we are blending, our children still deal with hard things every day. But without hard things, there would be no narrative. There would be no story to tell. Each of them has a story and they would tell it in their own way. Therefore, none of the opinions, advice, or beliefs that I share overshadows their right to see the world as they do.

Some of the events in this book are captured in photographs, like the night Jen and I got engaged, and the day of our wedding. These experiences are now the complicated silver lining of our recent past together. What can't be captured in pictures are the day-to-day struggles that persist; the grief, the trauma, the difficulty that change brings. Our relationships with each other and the challenges we face are filled with things that are quite common among families that are blending. Blending families is a process, not an event. Relationships are key—developing them, building them, and strengthening them. This book is a reflection of our experiences in coming together and in being together.

- *Justin Eller*

Acknowledgments

Our sincere thanks to those who spent untold hours giving support and offering encouragement in helping to make this project happen.

Sincere thanks to:

Tiffinie Wakely McAfee
Kristina Anderson
Nancy J. Miles
Shauna Packer
Heather Moore
Michele Holmes
Shanda Cottam
Tiffany Shumway
Melissa Dalton Martinez
Angela Eschler
Lara Stice Palmer
Holly Price-Banford
Matt & Lisa McClean
Colby & Julia Eller
Jenn Hudgins
Austin & Hailey Guymon
Cathy Sargent

JUSTIN AND JENNIFER ELLER

Lisa LaDow
Kathy Splawn
Russell J. Butler
Mike & Sienna Von Gunten
Lynn & Dianne Johnson
Paul Cardall
and
our children

Introduction

My wife Jen and I have worked together in providing detailed experiences and advice about life after being widowed. Our intention in writing this book is to help establish more dialogue in the broader LDS culture about how to work through the trauma of losing loved ones, beginning again, and blending families.

Losing a spouse can feel like you've lost direction in your life. This loss of *direction* is not the same as a loss of *purpose*. That's why we continue to press forward. To feel that life has blown off course is an *understatement*, but it doesn't mean that it has to be an *end statement*. The reality that we thought we would have is not the reality that we do have. In the book of Romans, speaking of trials and hardship, the Apostle Paul said that "tribulation worketh patience; And patience, experience; and experience, hope" (Romans 5:3–4, King James Version). As we have faith in God, hope is a blessing that gives us strength.

Together, Jen and I have seven children—their ages at the time we were married in July of 2017 were: Noel, age 19; Colby, 17; Shay, 13; Marie, 18; Ashlee,

15; Grant, 13; and Kate, 10. Before Jen and I met, we had already experienced losing a spouse as our children had experienced losing a parent. Being an only parent is a difficult task. We will discuss some of our personal challenges in parenting early on in this book.

Both of our families have different backgrounds and we both started out as complete strangers. Our story together began when Jen and I started dating. As our relationship progressed we met each other's children and at a certain point, our children met each other. Many issues arose when we announced to our children that we would be getting married. Perhaps they recognized that there were more difficult changes on the horizon. If so, they assumed correctly.

Blending families is not easy. It requires every family member to take a leap of faith. It's been a new kind of hard for each of us. We have our trials and we have our triumphs. Despite the everyday challenges there comes an ensuing hope that we are all in the right place at the right time. That each of us has a place in the plan of happiness and that being together is an integral part of it. Ours is a story of hope. We're living it, and we want to share it with you.

PART 1

Hard Times

CHAPTER 1

The Catalyst of Bereavement

Difficult roads often lead to beautiful destinations.
—*Zig Ziglar*

Jen's Story

In March of 2016, my late husband Stoney Winterton took his life. Our twentieth anniversary was just six days away. Stoney was a well-known, well-loved man in our community of South Jordan, Utah. He was very service-oriented and had a way of making people feel welcome and appreciated. He was at the height of his career, and from the outside it looked like he had it all. But our marriage was far from perfect. He had struggled with addiction for nearly all our married life. Our children did not know about his addiction, so the knowledge of his struggles and any marital differences between us were new to them, making it more devastating when tragedy struck. I'll never forget the day when the detective came to our house and confirmed that my husband had committed suicide. I remember the confusion and devastation that came over me. The pain was not just mental and emotional—it was also physical.

The night before Stoney took his life, he had arrived home from a business trip. We'd missed him, as he had been gone for several weeks. Our children happily gathered around him and listened to the stories he told about his latest trip. On the following morning, our family was preparing to attend the dedication of the Provo City Center Temple, but before we left for the church, Stoney was nowhere to be found. To the shock of our family and the local community, Stoney Winterton took his life on March 20, 2016. He left us with many unanswered questions, some of which may never be answered in this life.

Within days of Stoney's passing, I was planning a funeral before I could even comprehend what had happened. I thought to myself, "Is this real? Is he really gone?" In the first few weeks after his passing, I remained in a state of shock. It was hard to eat, sleep, and care for my kids. I remember telling them, "I will never leave you. It's going to be okay!" Many close family members stayed by my side.

One day in particular, when I was trying to provide comfort for one of my children who was struggling, I told a close friend, "I don't know if I can do this." I said of my kids, "It's impossible to hold up their four hearts while I am struggling with the pain that's still in mine.

I can't do it alone." She let me express my feelings of hopelessness as I explained that I hadn't really internalized my feelings yet. I'll always remember her answer. "Jen," she said, "you don't have to do it alone. The only one that can feel exactly what you feel is the Savior. He's the one that can lift the burden and heal your heart. You can't do it alone, and you aren't expected to. Your kids already have a Savior. You need to be their mother and point them toward the Master to heal what is broken. Just help them come to know the Savior."

In a biblical story found in the book of Daniel, King Nebuchadnezzar creates a golden image and commands everyone to worship it. Anyone who was not found worshipping it was to be thrown into a fiery furnace. Shadrach, Meshach, and Abednego refused to worship the king's false god. The king was furious, and the three were thrown into the fiery furnace, yet they received no harm. As the king observed what was taking place, he said, "Lo, I see four men loose, walking in the midst of the fire, and they have no hurt; and the form of the fourth is like the Son of God" (Daniel 3:25). We learn that the Savior was not standing outside the hot, fiery furnace offering help and comfort to the three. He was inside, standing right next to them. He is there for us in the hardest moments. Always.

Justin's Story

My late wife Angie was a skilled PICU nurse at UC Davis Medical Center in Sacramento, California. She was an avid runner and was very health conscious.

In early January of 2014, Angie ran a half marathon with ease. Just two months later she went to the doctor because she'd had a dry, hacking cough for quite some time. Within forty-eight hours we learned that one of her lungs had collapsed and fluid had filled her chest cavity. Her right lung was a shrunken mass of tumors, and the cancer had already metastasized to other regions in her body. It was stage 4 nonsmokers' lung cancer. The doctor who bore the news to us said it was a case of very back luck. Indeed it was, and we may never know the cause of her cancer.

I felt the hurt of watching my children try to understand the *when*, the *how*, and the *why* as we supported her and stayed by her side during her sixteen-month battle with cancer. *When* did the cancer begin to grow in her lungs? The cancer had reached stage 4 in medical terminology before it was discovered. *How* did she get cancer when she was so healthy and took such great care of her body? Finally, *why* did she have to get cancer? Angie was only thirty-nine years old when she was diagnosed.

I tended to Angie the best I could throughout her sixteen months of chemotherapy and radiation treatment, striving to provide her with comfort. There were many nights, even in her depleted state, that she would spend extra time on her knees by the bedside, pleading with her Heavenly Father, asking him to grant her more time to be with our family. There was no anger or bitterness. Angie just wanted to live. She wanted to beat cancer. She explored every viable resource that could help her. But after ten months of effective treatment, the cancer began spreading throughout her body again. And within another six months, it claimed her life.

Angie once expressed her deepest concern about what would happen to our family if she were to pass away. She was afraid that I wouldn't be able to handle raising our three children alone. Her concerns were substantiated by the fact that I live with Bipolar Type 1, which at times has been debilitating. She had spent years working to keep our family together in the wake of my diagnosis. She asked me to promise her that I would raise our kids and not leave it to anyone else. I promised her that I would have the strength to raise our children.

The night she passed away, she knew the fight was over. She accepted that her time on earth had been somehow predetermined for reasons that we could not understand. Angie passed away on August 6 of 2015, holding our three children close to her as I stood at the foot of her bed, rubbing her feet, watching the sorrow in the eyes of our children as she passed from the visual side of the veil to the spiritual realm of the place that we call paradise. Looking back, I remember my dad saying, "I've seen many people die, but she was as beautiful in death as she was beautiful in life." She was calm, and with dignity she was prepared to meet her Savior. With her passing, we became what felt like a broken family, and our lives were forever changed.

After her passing, I felt a weight that seemed unbearable at times, but I bore it because I needed to, I wanted to, and because I had to. There were still children to be taken care of and raised. When I became an only parent,

I felt a guilt of inadequacy every day. Bereavement in and of itself is heavy, and the day-to-day act of trying to be enough for my kids was difficult. My moods took me to dark places for months at a time. I call the dark times a "blackout period." It is a time when you can hardly remember the short-term details of just about anything. People would tell me I was doing great. But I wasn't. My emotional strength began to dwindle, as did my spiritual perspective. I constantly prayed that my struggles would not add to my children's struggles and that their spiritual perspectives would not be hindered by my shortcomings. I prayed for help with finding medications that would stabilize my moods and for help in parenting my children properly. Perhaps I felt as if my broken heart was accompanied by a broken mind. Elder Jeffrey R. Holland explains, "Broken minds can be healed just the way broken bones and broken hearts are healed. While God is at work making those repairs, the rest of us can help by being merciful, nonjudgmental, and kind" ("Like a Broken Vessel," 42). As my focus was on my own health and the health and welfare of my children, I found that when we looked deep inside ourselves, amazing things could take form as we were being shaped by our experiences.

CHAPTER 2

The Pain of Loss

Joy always comes after sorrow.

—Henry B. Eyring

The northern lights (aurora borealis) are a natural light display in the earth's sky, predominantly seen in the high-latitudinal regions of the North Arctic. They project a brilliant array of colors in the night sky. Essentially, the northern lights are a natural phenomenon of ethereal beauty that has dazzled the eyes of mankind for ages. It's been said by observers that these lights in the heavens can help put life into perspective. However, in order to see them, you must travel approximately two thousand miles north of the mainland United States, to Fairbanks, Alaska. Even so, the northern lights come and go as they please, so there is no guarantee that they will arrive when you do. Even when they do appear, they can be difficult to see. But if you're willing to be diligent and to brave the subfreezing air long enough, at some point you will see them.

The journey to see the northern lights has many parallels to life after loss. Many of us yearn for a sign from the heavens that everything will ultimately work out. For some, the arduous journey of bereavement begins with a terminal diagnosis like cancer. For others, bereavement begins suddenly—when a loved one dies unexpectedly. Regardless of how we've experienced loss, the trials are real. And just as the northern lights can be difficult to see even after all the struggles of getting to the right place, the Lord's plan for us can also be difficult to see. But with faith, we can realize that the Lord often blesses us in ways that we may fail to recognize at first glance. I think of loss as a "walk through the valley of the shadow of death" (Psalms 23:4). It's lonely and can feel cold like the frigid air of the North Arctic as we pray for our heavenly lights to appear in their splendor. This doesn't mean that we won't receive the blessings that the Lord promises to send us. The blessings are there, but it is up to us to ask, recognize, and claim them. The greatest of these blessings is the gift of *hope*! Our own northern lights will display themselves at some point, and then we can know that it is hope that has brought us to a place of understanding. Just like the northern lights, hope can put our lives into perspective.

When a person becomes widowed, everything customary changes. Upon waking in the morning, we look to the other side of the bed and nobody's there. For a moment, we forget everything that has happened. Then, becoming fully awake, memories flash through the mind. We might ask ourselves, "Is this all real?"

Then comes the re-realization that our partner is not gone for the day, but gone for life.

How nice it would be if we could just have one glimpse of our deceased loved one. How nice it would be if we could just speak with them again. There are so many things to say and questions we'd like to ask. And when the children share the same longing, it's difficult to watch. We can console them, and pray that consolation is enough. At times, it may seem that the pain will never end. But there is always hope. As President Dieter F. Uchtdorf tells us, "Hope will open your eyes to the happiness that is placed before you" ("A Summer with Great-Aunt Rose," 19).

As widows and widowers, we long to understand the purposes of God's plan for us, for our children, and for our deceased partner. There is comfort in knowing that the heavens are not closed. It may feel at times that we are in the midst of a two-thousand-mile trek as we continue on. Indeed, the changes affect every aspect of our lives we wonder how life could have, would have, or should have been. Sometimes the sadness can be so strong that a successful day consists of getting out of bed in the morning, taking a shower, and putting on freshly washed clothes. There are also times when complete isolation is preferable because it feels too difficult to put on a friendly smile. We've all been there, and it's okay.

Amidst our struggles in life, one question we might ask ourselves is: "How far am I willing to go to see the glory of the heavens and understand Heavenly Father's plan for me and my family?" We once had a picture of the way life would be, and suddenly our picture was changed. It is important to remember that although your journey in life may be running a different course, it is still *your* journey. And hope can lighten your way.

Seeking Approval

The Lord is concerned with the matters that we are concerned with. When my late wife Angie died, I began seeking her approval about how I was raising our children. I'd break out in tears and speak to her as if she were there. I would say things like, "I'm doing the best I can, but the kids are struggling, and so am I." My children wanted to dream about Angie, but they didn't. But I had several dreams in which Angie would tell me things like, "Tell the kids that they are doing well," which I did tell them.

Then, on a particular night about fourteen months after Angie's passing, I had a lucid dream, and she was there. I was dreaming, and I knew I was dreaming. I could see Angie and communicate with her. She said, "You're dreaming." I replied, "I know I'm dreaming." To my surprise, she told me to quit seeking her approval about how I was raising the kids. She then said, "Seek the approval of the Lord." When I woke up, I could remember my dream clearly, as if we'd just been talking to each other, and for the first time since her passing, I didn't feel hollow.

Through this experience, I learned the simplest and yet the most powerful truth that I could comprehend at that time. I needed to direct my children to seek the Lord's help for healing and do the same for myself. At that time, I also came to an understanding that Angie was on the other side of the veil exercising her faith, continuously praying that our family would learn through the Spirit that she was there. That she was near. And that there would be times that we could feel her presence.

The Wrestle with God

When I started wrestling in high school, it always amazed me how exhausted I would get after three one-minute rounds. Sometimes I would get so tired that I'd rather have somebody pin me so that the match would be over than continue to do my best to win. Wrestling requires conditioning for physical strength and stamina. When opponents square off, it's a show of combined strength and balance. The best wrestlers were the ones that pushed themselves in practice and never took the easy way out.

In a spiritual sense, a wrestle with God requires conditioning and great exertion prior to seeing and understanding Heavenly Father's plan. When we experience loss, it's tempting to forsake our spiritual conditioning. If we become bitter, the efforts that we must make to get back into spiritual conditioning are much more difficult. But even in our weakest state, it is never too late to come back. The spiritual act of wrestling requires prayer, fasting, and good works. Praying on a whim is not enough to see and understand the blessings that God is showering upon us without reservation.

The concept of wrestling with God is explained in the book of Alma as it states, "Nevertheless Alma labored much in the spirit, wrestling with God in mighty prayer, that he would pour out his Spirit upon the people" (Alma 8:10). By exercising faith, we can discover spiritual gifts that we never knew we had. We can see things that we never thought possible. We can understand that even if our path takes twists and turns that we never anticipated, the destination is still the same.

We will discuss dating in a later chapter, but I want to point out that while dating, Jen and I had a long-distance relationship, so we had to maximize our time with each other and with each other's children. I lived in Lincoln, California, and she lived in South Jordan, Utah. The distance between her house and mine was 637 miles. On her first visit to California, she and I prepared a nice meal for us and my three kids to enjoy. As it was my first serious dating experience, my children were not very welcoming. Jen was a stranger to them. There was an awkward silence at the dinner table. Jen and I both made an effort to have dinner time discussions but to little avail.

As we finished dinner, Jen suddenly burst with enthusiasm and said, "All right! Who wants to arm wrestle?" The kids were taken a bit off guard, and yet they all agreed with the idea. Jen positioned herself on the carpet and asked, "Who's first?" Colby laid down facing Jen. The rest of us watched as she pushed Colby's arm down to the floor. Shay was next, and although Jen gave her a chance for a moment, Jen easily won. Next up was Noel, who I'd assumed would win the match, as athletic as she is. Although there was a slight struggle,

Jen beat her. We laughed together for the first time. But by this time, I was a little nervous because Jen had shown that she was strong and I had to arm wrestle her next. So I used my usual excuse. "Okay," I said, "it's my turn, but I'm left-handed." It's something I've always said before an arm wrestle so as to make it clear that if I lose with my right arm, it doesn't mean that my opponent is stronger than me. They must beat me with both arms to claim victory.

In reality, I don't know which of my arms is stronger. I've just always assumed that the arm that I prefer to use is the stronger of the two. I've always favored my left arm and given it my best effort. But this doesn't mean that my greatest strength is in my left arm. I've always made the assumption that *preference* is strength. But I'm happy to say I won the arm wrestle with both arms.

This experience taught me more than just that Jen was a good arm wrestler. I realized at that time how often we make spiritual assumptions based on preference. Our current belief systems could be holding us back from recognizing the spiritual gifts that the Lord is waiting to bless us with—gifts that may bless the lives of those around us, especially our children. Just as with talents, spiritual gifts must first be realized by having an open heart, an open mind, and by our efforts of faith in asking the Lord to help us identify them. Most often, these gifts are not a matter of our personal preference as much as the preference of he who knows us best. We all have strengths and weaknesses; however, if we jump to conclusions and never allow ourselves to be tested, we might never know where some of our true strengths lie. In the end, we may find that through our match of wrestling with God, he has matched it with a spiritual embrace.

The Stories We Tell Are the Stories We Live

Widows and widowers all have different stories, but the one thing we all have in common is that we've endured the heartbreak that only the widowed know. As I've been in support groups online and met others who are widowed at conferences and workshops, it's evident that we have been stretched to what we feel are our limitations. At times, we may need to lean on the strength of others. Indeed, we all have a wrestle before God, and as we pray for strength, he holds nothing back in blessing our lives and the lives of our children. As we are conditioned in our trials, we have opportunities to develop understanding, compassion, and empathy through the hardships that we do and will endure.

We might look around and see families that seem to be more complete. We need not envy nor feel that our family is irrevocably broken. We all possess strengths that might never have been known had the circumstances been different. Much like gifts, strengths are blessings from God, but we must be willing to accept that it is in the act of "wrestling" that we receive such blessings.

These strengths often appear *while* we are being tried by difficult circumstances. In the book of Ether, it says, "For if they humble themselves before me, and have faith in me, then will I make weak things become strong unto them" (Ether 12:27). Humility, rather than preference, faith, rather than preference, put us into a place where the Lord can point us to and magnify our true strengths.

Considerations

♡ Are you aware of the blessings that God sends us that can put our circumstances into perspective? Do you acknowledge it?

♡ Have you thought of temple attendance since the passing of your spouse? It may feel awkward at first without your significant other, but it is a sure way to receive spiritual strength and guidance.

♡ Are you taking care of your own basic needs along with the needs of your family? Be kind to yourself, nobody knows what you're going through except you.

CHAPTER 3

Comfort in Mourning

One of the hardest lessons in life is letting go. Whether it's guilt, anger, love, loss, or betrayal. Change is never easy. We fight to hang on and we fight to let go.

—*Mareez Reyes*

Jen

On the morning Stoney passed, word got around quickly, and people were rushing to help our family. Sympathy notes, uplifting quotes and writings, financial support, and many other gifts and generous offerings filled our home. Because Stoney was so well known and loved, the news of his death was devastating not just to my family but to the many others that knew him. People wanted to help comfort the kids and me. Many family and friends were there at just the right times when we needed them.

In the first couple of days, we had a sign posted on the door stating that I was resting but so appreciated them coming by to express their love. People would sign their names and leave gifts of various kinds. It touched my heart each night to read the names of people who had come that day and to know the love and sympathy they expressed.

My children were also touched by acts of generosity. The organizations of the extracurricular activities that my kids were involved in also reached out to us expressing their support. My oldest daughter, Marie, was the captain of her high school golf team. She received an outpouring of love by way of visits and notes. The golf team also canceled their participation in a tournament that coincided with the date of Stoney's funeral so that they could be in attendance.

My second daughter, Ashlee, had just made the high school drill team two days before her dad's passing. The coach barely knew her, but she, the parents, and her teammates brought a beautiful quilt that they made in her team colors. My son Grant was playing baseball at the time. It was the closest connection he and his dad shared together. It was tough for him to keep playing, but he dug in and never missed a game. At the end of the season, he received a special award given for his great attitude and for not giving up!

Kate was just two weeks shy of her ninth birthday when Stoney died. He'd planned his upcoming business trips so that he could be home for her birthday. As the day approached, she had moments of anxiousness and tears. She wanted her "big, strong dad" back. I was in no condition to throw a birthday party, so the mothers of her friends threw a surprise party for her. They invited me and my other kids to be there and watch her arrive. As she walked in with swollen eyes and heavy shoulders, her countenance changed to brightness, and a smile returned to her face. She was surprised, happy, and grateful. And I was overflowing with a sense of gratitude that was impossible to put into words. I believe that through these experiences, my children have developed a greater capacity for love and compassion toward those in need.

One special experience the first week after Stoney died was that the neighbors tied yellow ribbons on every tree and mailbox lining the streets on both sides of our neighborhood and as far out as the boundaries of our congregation extended. I remember coming down my stairs one afternoon and seeing my children peer out the window watching their friends, leaders, and neighbors of all ages cutting and fastening the ribbons to the trees. Tears welled up in their eyes seeing the people they knew and loved ornamenting the trees. The ribbons remained up until after his funeral.

Stoney had business associates from around the globe. Many wanted to help in some way. I was astonished at the love that was shown us. There were ordinary people doing extraordinary things. At the two-month anniversary of his passing, I was troubled as to how I could ever thank each individual who had touched our lives. I wanted people to know how I felt about the kind service they gave so freely. I had been very reclusive in dealing with grief and trauma—I had spent my energy on planning the funeral and doing the necessary things when someone passes.

I had begun counseling with a therapist and expressed to him my desire to thank everyone who had helped and encouraged my family during those difficult times. He suggested that I go on social media to say the things I was thankful for. I knew that it was not expected, but I wanted to acknowledge that their kindness had lifted our spirits. They wanted us to feel their love. I took his advice and I posted the following:

Two months ago today we lost a huge piece of our family as he passed from this life unexpectedly. In my own life experience, my heart has never experienced such shattered devastation, a loss with such deep pain to the point of physical suffering. It was as if my heart was literally bleeding inside my chest. Stoney's death has left a hole so big in my heart, my children's hearts, and for so many of you who loved him too. He was a friend to all who knew him, and he loved everyone. To say we miss him every day is insufficient in describing our feelings. He truly was a gift to our family and to everyone he knew. The weight of moving forward and making our way without him has been a daily, and sometimes an hourly, struggle.

But, along with the pain, I have felt my heart fill with gratitude to the point that I felt it would burst. The outpouring of love, charity, assistance, service, gifts, acts of kindness, and so many more offerings that I cannot list have been given to me and my children. They've come from family and friends near and far, but also from people around the world that Stoney had business associations with.

It has helped us not to bear such a huge weight alone. I would love to write a personal thank-you to each and every one of you who has helped us in any way, big or small, but that would be a near-impossible task. I want to express my gratitude to everyone who has and is continuing to help us bear this tragedy and loss. Please know that nothing goes unnoticed or unappreciated. Miracle after miracle happens in our family. Our hearts are so full amid our pain BECAUSE of all of you! You are angels on earth who have rushed to our aid, and we are so thankful. I'm grateful for the knowledge and peace that we will see Stoney again. And that this life is not the end. I will forever be grateful for the Atonement of Jesus Christ. We love you! With love, Jen and the kids.

Justin

When my late wife, Angie, was diagnosed with stage 4 lung cancer, her coworkers, friends, and family members began to shower us with support. She had been a PICU nurse at UC Davis Medical Center for more than ten years of her career. As she was now a patient at the hospital that she was employed at, nurses and doctors came to her room bearing gifts and expressing their concern and love for her and our family. Church members in the Lincoln, California area held a special fast for her. I was amazed at how many people were inspired by the strength she showed in going through the harsh chemotherapy and radiation treatments. People wanted to help her by any means possible. In short, the floodgates of compassion were opened, and she received many acts of service and kindness.

The nurses in her unit rallied around her and established a care fund called "Team Angie" to help with the expenses of her treatment. Members of our ward came and visited her, expressing their support. Priesthood leaders came, and the Relief Society arranged to have meals delivered to our home every evening. An outpouring of caring was expressed both by people we knew and by people we'd never met.

Many memories come to mind of a willingness to comfort those in mourning. One night, while we were at home having dinner, the doorbell rang. When I answered the door, there was a plastic bag filled with money on our doorstep, but no one was there. This gesture of kindness was an anonymous gift. After finding out that it was given to us by the children of a particular family that lived down the street from us, tears filled my eyes as I saw Angie smiling with gratitude in her heart. In Angie's words as posted on social media, she said:

> Truly touched by someone's generosity! Got doorbell ditched tonight and found an envelope of money and a note obviously written by a child. It looks like some child/children gave us money they had earned themselves. That is one of the sweetest things I've ever seen. Thank you so much, whoever you are!

Becoming a Gracious Receiver

After a loss, there is no shame in relying on the strength of others to help us through hard times. Receiving service graciously allows others the blessings of providing service. There seems to be a crossroad along the path of bereavement where a decision must be made. There are two distinct responses that can permanently affect a person's life. On the one hand, it can increase one's ability to recognize the sweet, where on the other hand, one can develop bitterness toward God about the circumstances that are a result of what we've lost. However, these responses are within our control and can change at any time. Our reaction to loss has a lot to do with whether or not we trust that the Lord will make things right, which he promises he will do. Recognizing the sweet sometimes means that we are willing to receive the love and support that is willingly shown by others.

I'd never felt that I could be a good caretaker until circumstances challenged that idea. I had always gladly accepted the stereotype that men aren't good nurturers. When my late wife Angie was battling cancer, I took on the role of caretaker, and looking back I know that Angie felt I did well because she told me so. When she passed away, I became the sole caretaker of my children. I had some help getting started. I was serving in the Elder's quorum presidency, and the other members of the presidency were readily available to be there when I needed them. Family friends helped me to understand more of what my children were going through and what their needs were. I learned how to cook a meal for the entire family (and I don't mean I just warmed up Hot Pockets and said, "Here's your dinner"). My parents came over weekly to check on us and to make sure that my children and I were fed a good Sunday dinner. With the help of my mom, I learned how to grocery shop. With the help of others, I was actively doing things that I never thought that I'd do.

Considerations

♡ Do you recognize the scope of your support base? You are not alone.

♡ If you are overwhelmed, are you willing to accept the service that is graciously given by others?

♡ Is there a way to express appreciation for the kindness of others even if you can't reach out to everyone individually?

CHAPTER 4

Understanding and Coping with Grief

Tears come from the heart and not from the brain.
—*Leonardo da Vinci*

Tears are an interesting phenomenon. They come from what we are feeling rather than what we are seeing. I like to think of tears as raindrops because they come and go. They are first buried deep in the heart before they are seen in our eyes. At times, there can be dark clouds of sorrow. The darkness can be depressing, but it doesn't always have to be. The body is meant to feel. Crying is a natural thing. We can recognize our grief, experience it, and at some point, let it go if that's what we choose to do.

When clouds of sorrow collide with clouds of mourning, and with clouds of loneliness, and all the other feelings that classify grief, a storm arises in the heart that may produce a flash flood of tears intemperately flowing so rapidly that it feels like the storm will never end. But the storm does come to an end as the emotions let up, and soon the view of fresh sunlight peeks through as if to say, "This too shall pass." The grief that in so many ways entrenches us is just on the other side of joy. Elder Jeffrey R. Holland once said, "Even if you cannot always see that silver lining on your clouds, God can, for He is the very source of the light you seek. He does love you, and he knows your fears. He hears your prayers. He is your Heavenly Father, and surely He matches with His own the tears His children shed" (*Created for Greater Things* [2011]).

There may be tears of bitterness, as well as tears of sweetness. Tears of depravity can become tears of renewal. Tears of displacement can become tears of enlargement. Tears of commiseration can become tears of compassion. Tears of misunderstanding may beget tears of understanding. And as there are tears of emptiness, there will in time come tears of reunion, accompanied by tears of joy. Yes, even joy! Just as Jesus wept with a fullness of joy when he was among the faithful Nephites, we are assured that we too can experience such joy as we become like him. In truth, not all storms come to disrupt your life; some come to clear your path. In reality, crying is healthy; it's like meeting adversity face-to-face and becoming friends with it.

There is a recent study in a book called *The Topography of Tears* by Rose-Lynn Fisher. Fisher is a photographer who wanted to find out if tears that are triggered by our different emotions are all made of the same molecules. Through a digital high-resolution optical scope, she photographed dried tears that were caused by different emotions. Fisher explains that "It's as though each one of our tears carries a microcosm of the collective human experience, like one drop of an ocean." The photographs of tears that came from emotions such as sadness and depression had many rigid, geometric shapes, while tears associated with happier emotions had more organic and rounded shapes. Tears of change and tears of reunion were also shown to have unique features. This study suggests that not all tears are alike. It is therefore believed that, based on their origin, tears have some of their own distinct features.

While the study of tears is in its infancy, one conclusion that may be drawn could be despite the fact that most tears originate in the heart, they all have different properties according to the human experiences that cause them. Even in our sorrows, having a good cry may be beneficial to our health. Therefore, in the arena of bereavement, what should be worrisome is if we don't cry any tears at all.

To illustrate this point, my son Colby took his mother's diagnosis and death so severely that he thought he could never be happy again. He'd never cried even when things were at their worst. I had assumed that he was stronger than any of us because of maturity and that he was handling everything in a way "that a man should."

The flaw in my thinking was that he wasn't a man. He was just a boy. And men cry too. I know that I do. After his mom passed away, I realized that Colby was struggling more than any of us were. His grades in school had plummeted, and he began to isolate himself from others. As I talked to him, he confided in me that he couldn't cry even though he wanted to.

One day, while I was reading a Church publication called *Ensign*, the Spirit prompted me to start praying that Colby would have an experience that would help him amidst his struggles. My heart ached for him. I wanted him to have a dream or an experience that would comfort him and tell him that everything would be okay. I wept at that moment, not realizing that he was upstairs in his room pleading with the Lord to give him understanding. We were unknowingly praying for the same thing at the same time. As I concluded my prayer, I could hear him coming downstairs crying.

He told me that he'd been praying for an experience that he might know that his mother Angie was proud of him and that she was aware of the pain he was feeling. The Spirit spoke to him so strongly that he was able to cry for the first time since his mother's initial diagnosis of cancer. For the first time in two years, those pent-up emotions of pain and sorrow poured from his eyes. His tears soon became tears of gratitude and relief. He'd finally had a moment that filled his heart with joy. We wept together.

One of the greatest difficulties during the grieving process is that we can speak to our loved one as if they are here, but the assumption is that they aren't here to speak to us. We express how we feel about them, but they aren't here to listen to the things we are saying. While we know that they can communicate with us through the Spirit—we don't always know what they're hearing or saying. We talk about what they must be feeling and how they would want to be here, to touch us, speak to us, to hold us, to be with us. We know these things. Yet our communication with them must be taken on faith and felt through the promptings of the Spirit.

Listening for Understanding

Angie passed away just three days before Shay's twelfth birthday. As a family, we'd cried many tears throughout the process of seeing her health decline as she battled cancer. It had been a very traumatic summer. Within about a week of her passing, the school year began. It was hardly enough time for Shay to catch her breath. A couple of days into school, she came home with tears in her eyes. It was to be expected because she had just lost her mom. I hugged her tightly as tears rolled down her cheeks. I didn't expect her to explain why she was crying. Her mother had just passed away, so naturally she was grieving. But I felt like I needed to delve a little deeper to understand what concerned her.

"What are you feeling, honey?" I asked.

Her answer surprised me a bit, although it shouldn't have.

Her response was, "My teachers keep handing out papers and telling us to have our mom sign them. How am I supposed to do that?"

What I heard pained me as I held her in my arms. As a widower of about two weeks, I had learned my first lesson about the concept of grief triggers. A trigger is a reminder that brings back feelings of loss, and they can be many. In grieving a loss, triggers seem innumerable and can touch off a landslide of emotions, and the triggers will generally linger for months or years, if not for life.

Grief Stages, Triggers, and Individual Needs

Grief for the hurt of our children is real and can feel just as heartbreaking as the grief we have for our spouse who has passed. The pain of hearing our children in their bedrooms at night, mourning for the loss of their parent, rings a strong tone of sadness. We can see, and to some extent, we can feel their pain. Their grief is our grief. Just as with adults, the symptoms of grief differ from child to child, and they will manifest themselves in time, if not immediately following the passing of a parent. My children began the grieving process when their mother was diagnosed with cancer. It was intensified when she passed away.

Although we had Angie in our lives for another sixteen months, watching her suffering with chemotherapy and radiation treatments and the horror of seeing her health deteriorate brought additional hurt to all of us. As I mentioned before, my children and I were at the hospital the night she passed. I've often imagined what it would have been like if I were a child watching my mother die. It's nearly incomprehensible to me. It was hurtful to see the emotional pain that my children struggled with, and it is hurtful to see what they still struggle with. Now each of them has now had nightmares about her illness. They've often wondered why in their dreams she could not be the healthy mother that had raised them for so many years.

There are formulas laid out in the field of psychology about the "stages" of grief. Grief is said to have five stages: *denial, anger, bargaining, depression*, and *acceptance*. After Angie passed away, I took my children to a therapist who laid out these stages of grief in our first and only visit. My children were not ready to discuss the sadness that they were feeling at the time. But I do believe that therapy can be beneficial. I've gone through it by myself many times over the past few years.

Jen and I have found with both ourselves and with our children that there is no definitive universal success formula in tackling our challenges. The process of grief can come in various orders, and some stages that we thought were resolved might not be. It's unpredictable. I've found that the "stages" of grief can come at any time, in any order, and can revisit you again and again.

Acceptance is not the end of the difficulties of life without a spouse or a parent. Depression is real, and it can come to the forefront regardless of the stage of grief we are in. We are not all programmed in the same way. Everyone handles things differently. Grief is sometimes chaotic, and there is no sequential formula for overcoming it. There are numerous transitions in the path of healing, but there is not a definitive invitation for you to get your old life back. In reality, you can't get your old life back. But you can progressively move forward in healthy ways. Moving forward allows one to keep the great memories of the past, take all of the lessons learned from it, and continue on in the progression of your life.

Elder Joseph B. Wirthlin once said, "The Lord compensates the faithful for every loss. . . . Every tear today will eventually be returned a hundredfold with tears of rejoicing and gratitude" ("Come What May," 28). But there often lies a battle. Acceptance and hope can be binary feelings when we are grieving. Life can continue to be cruel, but as we persevere in faith, it's an understanding of God's plan that will ultimately make of our lives something precious and beautiful again. He conditions us to reach our full potential and helps us move toward becoming as he is: a being of truth and happiness forever. Through Christ there is healing. Through him there is purpose. The most effective way to heal is by accepting the healing he offers us.

Self-Care and Getting Support

Several years ago, Jen and I had the opportunity to speak and do workshops about remarriage and blending families at an LDS Widows/Widowers Conference in Mesa, Arizona. The workshops that were offered addressed many issues that widows and widowers face after the death of a spouse including Complicated Grief, Accessing the Atonement for Healing, Personal Finances, Parenting Approaches, and more.

At the luncheon, I looked over and saw a table in a corner of the cultural hall that offered health foods. Out of curiosity, I walked over to the table and sampled a few healthy snacks. I wasn't particularly fond of the taste, but the need to focus on physical health really resonated with me. I knew from personal experience that mental and physical health can rapidly decline at any stage of grief and trauma. The struggles for me weren't just due to having a poor diet and lack of exercise. But they contributed to them. I had also developed symptoms of deep depression and wasn't getting the proper sleep that I needed in order to function from day-to-day. I also knew that Jen dealt with similar challenges of depression and sleep deprivation caused by post-traumatic stress disorder (PTSD) as a result of the nature of her loss. I had witnessed it in the eight months that we had been married at the time.

As the luncheon ended, I took a moment to imagine myself hosting another workshop that dealt with mental and physical health, while passing around a jelly bean jar filled with Prozac to all who attended the workshop. Of course I would never do that, nor would it be appropriate. The reason such a silly image came to me is because the need to discuss the issue of psychological and physiological self-care (and getting professional support) is real. The topic can be a source of shame for some, but it shouldn't be.

In my experience, sometimes I've felt ashamed to admit how much I've been struggling to have faith in God. At times, I haven't taken into consideration that answers to my prayers could come from the help already available to me through friends, family, and health professionals. I have also realized that sometimes you can't just "pray it away," so to speak. Sometimes, the grief goes deep and can lead to temporary bouts of serious depression or other forms of illness. I've also realized that whether it be through medicine, homeopathic treatments, counseling, diet, or any other means of taking care of the body and mind, sometimes it's necessary to seek outside help in dealing with the challenges brought on by losing a spouse. It is not a sign of weakness to get help for such things. It is part of the self-care that can allow us to continue in our recovery. Remember that self-care is not a selfish act.

Considerations

♡ Are you aware of private support groups for widows/widowers, and remarried widows/widowers on Facebook? (See appendix for The Church of Jesus Christ of Latter-day Saints support groups for Widows and Widowers) Conferences are periodically held for members of these groups in some states.

♡ Have you considered grief counseling for you and/or your children? Note: Not all counselors are created equal.

CHAPTER 5

The Drama of Trauma

Trauma creates change you don't choose.
Healing is about creating change you do choose.

—*Michele Rosenthal*

I want to establish the fact that grief and trauma are not the same thing. Grief is caused by sorrow and mourning over a loss. Trauma is caused by distressing experiences that put the sufferer into a state of shock and cause psychological damage. However, both conditions can be present at the same time, which I believe is the most mental anguish that one could suffer in this life. Both grief and trauma can permanently change your mental and physical health. The act of mourning is deeply associated with grief, while trauma can make one feel anxiety, stress, fear of abandonment, and many more painful things that few can fully understand. Trauma feeds on one's vulnerabilities, produces vivid memories, and in some cases causes nightmares that can put the sufferer into a state of self-doubt, severe depression, and considerable fear.

Trauma can cause a mental illness called post-traumatic stress disorder (PTSD). It is often brought on by circumstances that are out of one's control, and the triggers for (PTSD) can cause instantaneous reactions. Post-traumatic stress disorder (PTSD) is not considered curable according to most health care professionals. It's important to note that trauma can be equally prevalent in children as it is in adults, and in many adults, their trauma has stemmed from childhood experiences. Fortunately, trauma is treatable through counseling, medicine, meditation, and a lot of love—especially in children. "The more healthy relationships a child has, the more likely he [or she] will be to recover from trauma and thrive. Relationships are the agent of change and the most powerful therapy is human love" (Bruce D. Perry, *The Boy Who Was Raised as a Dog* [2007]).

When I was in the sixth grade, the graduating classes of my elementary school set out for an exciting field trip before graduation. The destination was to be a theme park in the Bay Area of Northern California. My friends and I were so excited; we had anticipated the trip all year. On the bus ride there I remember hearing students in the back of the bus singing "Ninety-Nine Bottles of Beer on the Wall" over and over again. My friends and I talked about rides that we would or wouldn't go on. All the boys bragged and said they would go on anything.

We were just a couple of freeway exits away from the theme park when tragedy struck. There was a stalled rig with a semi-trailer in our path that the school bus driver did not see until it was too late. There was no time to avoid a collision. Our school bus hit the semi-trailer head-on. I remember hearing the screeching of brakes and the thunderous sound of colliding metal and breaking glass. Every row of seats in the bus was ripped from the floor and thrust toward the front. The semi-trailer was heavy, as it was filled to capacity with one-gallon cartons of milk, which burst and spilled into the wreckage. I got up and clasped my hands so that I could know whether or not I was dreaming. It was not a dream; it was real. Dozens of my classmates were hemmed in at the front of the bus, pinned down by the seats and the crumpled steel that was shaped by the force of the impact.

One of my classmates lost his life, and at least a dozen students were critically injured. The fire department quickly arrived at the scene of the accident. I looked up at the mangled wreckage and saw firefighters working meticulously in an effort to pull several students out of the debris. The students that were seriously injured were taken by ambulance or airlifted to a hospital in San Jose. I watched students being carted on cots into ambulances. Each ambulance driver quickly turned on their sirens and sped away until there were no ambulances left at the scene. I walked over to a place where most of the uninjured students had congregated next to a chain-link fence on the side of the freeway. Nobody knew where we were supposed to go.

Then, within a short time, an empty school bus pulled off the freeway and stopped next to us. A volunteer parent instructed us to get on the bus so that we could be taken to the hospital and be checked for injuries. As the bus doors opened, I could hear one of my classmates say, "I'm not getting on that!" We were terrified—none of us wanted to get on the bus. Every student was feeling instant trauma and fear of buses. Some of the students were crying and said they refused to go. But there was no other way to get so many people to the hospital. Many students were reluctant and fought it, but eventually, we all got on the bus and made it to the hospital where each of us was examined for injuries.

My sense of reality was changed that day. I would later realize that buses were a trigger for me. The thoughts that would come into my mind were that school buses were a sign of danger. A week following the bus accident was graduation day at the elementary school. Part of the graduation program consisted of watching short video clips of fellow students who were still in the hospital. What was meant to be a day to celebrate had become a day of sadness.

I spent a lot of time with my friend James that summer. Neither of us had sustained serious injuries from the accident, but one thing was certain; we experienced the mental trauma of reliving the accident over and over again in our young minds. Just riding in a car was frightening to us, but neither of our parents took it seriously at the time.

One day that summer, James's mom was driving us to my house. She thought it would be funny to scare us, so she pulled into an empty lot at a park close by. For

reasons I'll never understand, she started driving errati-
cally, doing figure eights. James and I begged her to stop
because we were scared. His mom was grinning and his
brothers were laughing at us as we started crying. With
each sharp turn, we yelled that we wanted to get out of
the car. It was terrifying to us. That night when I went
to bed, my mind took me back to the scene of the bus
accident. The sights and sounds flooded into my mind
as it replayed the memories of that day.

I share this story because such is the nature of
trauma. It's an isolating feeling of fear that people fail
to understand unless they've lived it with you. Even so,
it manifests itself in different ways for different people,
the same way that grief does. In this case, I didn't even
know I had it until years later.

Jen

Instant Trauma

On the Sunday morning that Stoney took his life,
none of us, neither my children nor me, knew of
any distress that was going on in his mind. All of us
were getting ready for church. He had showered, gotten
dressed, and gone down to the kitchen for breakfast.
Each of my children had seen him that morning, but
when it was time to get into the car and leave, he was
nowhere to be found. We discussed our conversations
with him that morning and discovered through Ashlee
and Marie that he had left on foot, headed east down
our street.

We searched but we could not find him. We sent texts and called his phone, but it was turned off. We drove through the neighborhood, but nobody had seen him or knew where he went. We were extremely worried, as this was not usual behavior for him. We figured there had to have been a logical explanation for it. But after about an hour, our fears began to escalate. The police, as well as family members, were contacted to help search for him. I returned home with the kids as others continued the search. About an hour later, a detective came to our door. He asked if he could talk to me somewhere in private. We went into the office. He said they'd found his body not far from home, by a ravine behind our neighborhood. He proceeded to tell me that Stoney had a self-inflicted gunshot wound that was fatal.

My brother and sister-in-law, who had arrived not long after the detective, went and informed my kids. I had gone into shock, and what added to it was that I could hear my kids screaming as they were told what had happened. The trauma was immediate, while the grief came later. I spent a lot of time in bed over the next couple of months while others tried to console me and care for my physical and emotional health. I can remember feeling such pain in my heart. Along with the emotional pain, I literally felt physical pain as if my heart was somehow pierced. The pain was constant and refused to subside. I could barely take a deep breath, and it was impossible to step aside and process what was happening around me. It was difficult to grasp that these unimaginable events had taken place—that they were real. It was equally hard to grasp that this had become the story that everybody knew us by.

Trauma can and does happen to many who have lost someone in a sudden, tragic way. In my case, it was the suicide of my husband and my children's father. Grief always appears when someone very close to you passes away. Trauma and PTSD can be added to grief when horrifying experiences are associated with death. There are no stages attached to trauma. It is what it is, and it would be ever present and never fade until my family and I began to address post-traumatic stress syndrome through extensive therapy.

Marie

Being Judged Wrongly

Whether we like it or not, people make choices that affect us in ways that we could never imagine. We feel the aftermath. When my dad passed away in 2016, I was absolutely crushed, the worst of it being that it was his choice to leave. While we are unable to change people's choices, we do control how we live afterward. In order to deal with the choice of my father, I started to see a counselor. Through extensive counseling, I got to a place where I was mentally capable of serving a mission for The Church of Jesus Christ of Latter-day Saints. I was called to serve in the Arizona Scottsdale Mission speaking Spanish, and the experiences I had there were unforgettable—the people I met, the testimony I established. Unfortunately, I had a traumatic experience that ended up causing me to be sent home after serving for only six months. When I got home, there were people who made comments and gave looks that made me feel as though I were worthless.

This wasn't the first time I had experienced feeling judged for the situation that I was in. It also happened when my father took his life. Most people I know have not had a family member commit suicide, so they don't understand. It is easy for people from the outside to judge, not knowing the real story and suffering within. With the death of my dad, there were no warning signs, no goodbye note, and no way to receive answers to countless questions. But people don't know this. People don't know that my dad left completely unexpectedly. They don't know that I physically watched him walk out of my life. The weight of, "Could I have stopped it, had I known what he was going to go and do?" is immense. Having people judge from the outside does not make that burden any lighter. I am now married to the most amazing man who has stood by me through the hardest times I have been through thus far. People have judged me from the outside and by my struggles since March 2016. Looking at me from the outside makes sense—the assumptions they make are understandable. But they don't know me. They don't know my struggles. They don't know my triumphs.

If I could give any advice to people who know of others struggling, suffering, or being affected by tragedy, it would be to not make assumptions. Do not judge. Judgment is ingrained into our human nature, but just because it's there doesn't mean we need to act on it. It hurts those on the receiving end. I can confirm that when people judge those struggling, it only hurts them more, especially when they are being judged for things out of their control.

Justin

The Panic Switch

Kate was just eight years old when her father took his life. Following the dreadful day of her father's passing, it became as if everything outside the ordinary structure of her understanding produced panic at the flip of a switch. She continued to flourish in routine activities but experienced anxiety if anything disrupted them.

One day, about a year into my marriage to Jen, as we were driving home from counseling Jen got a call from Kate. She was at home alone with a friend. She sounded startled as she said that a man had pulled up to the house in a white truck and started banging on the front door. Jen asked if the door was locked, and it wasn't. Kate then became frightened as she said, "He's coming into the house!"

Jen instructed Kate and her friend to go out the back door and walk to a neighbor's house. Jen quickly ended the call and dialed 911. She provided information to a dispatcher that we'd had a break-in. Kate called Jen again and said that the man had left the house carrying something and then he left. When we got home, three squad cars were parked in front of the house. As we got out of my truck, an officer approached us and asked if we had any cameras in the house that could have recorded the footage of what the man was doing there.

Jen told him that the only camera we had would start recording when someone rang the doorbell. But the suspect had only knocked on the door prior to entering the house. An officer was taking notes as Kate was telling him the details of the break-in. She said that a man had pulled up in a white truck, banged on the front door and entered the house. Shortly after, he left carrying something which he put in the front seat of his truck and then drove away. Jen and I went through the house looking for items that may have been stolen. I noticed that an Xbox was missing from Grant's bedroom.

I asked Jen, "Who would break into a house in broad daylight and just steal an Xbox? And how did he know where the Xbox was?"

Officers circled the neighborhood looking for a white truck, but they couldn't find one. Meanwhile, Jen was on the phone with Ashlee, asking her if she knew anybody that drives a white truck.

Ashlee replied, "No, but our friend Greg drives a red truck and came over to get his Xbox."

She continued, "He texted me and said that he was going to pick up his Xbox, and nobody was home, so I said he could go in the house and get it."

After hearing Ashlee tell the details, I asked Kate, "Are you sure the truck was white? Or was it red?"

Kate explained, "Well, I thought it was white, but it could have been red."

Mystery solved! We told Kate that she had done the right thing in calling us, but the details began to break down as she explained what happened. The suspect was not driving a white truck; he was driving a red one. The suspect was not a stranger but a friend of the family.

Such is the nature of trauma and (PTSD). When panic strikes, as it easily does, the details of reality can become blurry. The trauma response could be that the sufferer is reliving the events that caused them (PTSD) in the first place while struggling to be present. The sufferer generally has a very high startle response to possible danger. It's as if there is a panic switch that immediately moves from comfort to fear. (PTSD) is not the fault of the sufferer, and it could afflict anyone. Jen knew that Kate was traumatized by the alleged break-in, so she took Kate and her friend to buy a treat at the corner store. For Kate, candy is comfort. Unfortunately, for adults comfort is much more complicated than candy. But the triggers are so numerous that the shock factor almost seems like an inevitable response to anything that can't be controlled.

Several hours after the alleged break-in, everyone was calm and relaxed at home. Kate had her candy close by and a bowl of Fruity Pebbles in front of her. Marie was home watching over Kate. But the drama had only just begun. Jen and I were out on a date when we got a phone call from Marie. As Jen answered the phone, we could hear alarms resonating in the background. We could also hear Kate, and she sounded scared. Kate has an extreme fear of fire and fire alarms. Perhaps it's a fear of any kind of emergency or event that makes her feel like a situation might be out of her control.

Marie spoke calmly, "Hi, mom, the fire alarms are going off all over the house, and they won't turn off."

Jen said, "Okay, I'll call and make sure nobody sends the fire department."

Marie continued to provide comforting words to Kate. Jen quickly hung up and called Vivint to tell them not to dispatch the fire department. Unfortunately, the fire department had already dispatched two trucks to our house. To this day, I wonder what the neighbors must have thought, as we'd had a visit from just about every type of emergency response team that South Jordan had to offer in one day. If I'd have been an outsider looking in I would have thought to myself, "So that's what blending families looks like!"

Considerations

♡ There are clinically proven and time tested therapies to help victims of trauma. Are you aware of the types of therapies available?

♡ Trauma triggers are numerous and so are the symptoms. If you suffer from trauma, have you identified what your triggers are? Have you identified triggers in your children? How do you deal with them?

♡ What is your understanding of post-traumatic stress disorder (PTSD)? Is it possible that you could be suffering from (PTSD) due to complicated grief?

PART 2

Changing of the Seasons

CHAPTER 6

Deciding When to Begin Dating

*Hope gives us courage to do those things
that we don't believe we are capable of.*

—*Noelle Pikus Pace*

Being widowed and dating is complicated and can be confusing. Dating and remarriage are not the first nor the final answers to the dilemma of accepting a new beginning that often takes place after the loss of a spouse. Some feel the need to have a complete and total resolution *before* they begin dating. Some may choose to move more quickly and be working toward resolution *while* dating.

The concept of *where or when to begin* in the context of dating spans a myriad of personal triumphs that begins by continuing on with life after our partner passes away. Beginning again for me started with personal milestones I achieved in congruence with this new chapter of my life. I had turning points that I could identify and say, "Yes, this was a good day." This is not to say that I was no longer grieving. Rather, it was like taking my pulse to identify where my heart stood. I would ask myself, "Do I feel at peace with where my life is? Do I long for companionship? Am I ready to open my heart to love again?"

Beginning again for me also applied to restructuring and rebuilding my life by consciously adapting to the situations that I was facing from day to day. With regards to dating, I waited until I was able to make the transition from the "normal" life that I was once acquainted with, to the "new normal" life of dating and moving forward. As an adult who was widowed, it was tough to start dating, having spent the most precious moments in life with somebody that was now gone. I'd imagine that others have dealt with a similar struggle.

Adult dating is not easy, and there's no need to compare ourselves to others when it comes to when we start. The timeframe between suffering a loss and dating again need not be set by anyone else. It shouldn't be. Just as there should be no expectation for how long the grieving process takes, there should be no expectation as to how long you should wait to begin dating again. The transition process into the dating scene can be quite painful, or it can be a fulfilling experience, or it can be both.

How Did I Know I Was Ready to Date Again?

Jen

I want to emphasize that the most important words in this question are "I" and "date." For those who have become widowed, there is an adjustment period after losing a spouse. A period that may be several weeks, months, or even years. There is shock and confusion that your life as you thought it would go, or how you envisioned it, has blown off course. You might say to yourself, "I was supposed to grow old with my spouse! We had so many plans together!" In essence, the road you're on no longer looks the same as you'd expected it to look. You are forced to acclimate to a new life that you've involuntarily been placed into. It's abruptly reconfirmed at times. For example, you first awaken in the morning, and within seconds you remember what your new reality is. It's accurate to say that this transition period is quite different for everyone. There are an innumerable set of circumstances, and no two situations are alike. This is why I emphasize the word "I."

No one will know when you're ready to be involved in a relationship but you. You will know that you are ready when the idea of it speaks to you, not when you speak to it. I emphasize the word "date" because some widows will date, and yet some will never date again. The seasons of life, or where you are emotionally, physically, as well as mentally, may mean that you won't ever step foot on that path. And that is perfectly fine.

55

In my situation, given the rocky marriage I had experienced, I'd already decided to stay single. I would raise my children alone and be a great mom and grandma. That seemed safe. My late husband traveled very frequently for work. So naturally I thought for sure I could parent alone. I had been the primary one parenting already in many ways as it was. My focus was putting my time and energy into learning how to hear the Lord speak to me. I knew that when I needed help in guiding my kids, I'd be able to hear him. It was a rewarding time in developing my relationship with the Lord.

Then one evening in December of 2016, while on Facebook reading posts in a widows and widowers group, one post caught my eye. It was a list of encouraging quotes a widower had posted to lift others. My oldest daughter was struggling down at BYU her first semester away from home. She'd been suffering with the trauma related to her dad's sudden death. I was always looking for ways to help her. So, in that effort, I messaged the widower privately and asked for a more printable copy. That night we corresponded for hours, telling our stories and giving comfort when we discussed our challenges. The next day we continued communicating as we spoke in depth about our situations. Within just over a week, I wanted to meet Justin. He said that he'd be coming to Utah soon, and when the time came, we met each other for the first time.

Personally, I thought with all the scars I bore from the loss of trust, the betrayal I'd suffered, and PTSD, that I may have never been ready to say, "Okay. Now

I'm ready to date!" But I quickly realized that I was ready. It may happen that way for some. Like turning on a light switch in the mind. But the personal decision to date may be more subtle. And the beautiful thing about it is that it may find you before you find it. As you continue, perhaps a little unsteady on your feet at times, somehow there's a surety in your heart that says it's okay. You might pause and look side to side, but you just keep stepping forward, basking in the feeling that you are headed in the direction that's right for you.

Justin

About a month prior to meeting Jen, I received guidance that it was okay for me to start dating, although I loathed the thought of it. The immediate necessity, of course, was to continue raising my children the best I could and to teach them the best I knew how. I was forty-three years old, and my youngest child would be an adult by the time I turned forty-eight. The thought of being an empty nester at age forty-eight wearied me. I already felt lonely even though I still had kids in the house. So I knew that at some point I would date with true intention. However, my children were protective of me and were against the idea. I had prayed that when the time came to date that I would have their support, but when the time did come, their support didn't come automatically.

Before meeting Jen, I spent several days searching for gospel-related talks that counseled widows and widowers about dating and remarriage. Surprisingly, I found only a few gospel talks that directly addressed widows and widowers about the harsh realities of losing a spouse and what to expect from life after loss. After a lengthy search, I was able to find a talk that I could identify with. A short excerpt at the opening of the talk said, "Many widows and widowers wonder if they will ever feel alive again after the death of their beloved companions. But surviving spouses from around the world bear witness that there is life after the death of a loved one and that a loving Father in Heaven will help provide the way to move forward" (Campbell, "Widows and Widowers," 54).

For the first time, I began to understand what the concept of moving forward meant. I learned that moving forward is different than moving on. When I decided that I wanted to date Jen, it was a tough predicament because my kids still interpreted moving forward the same way that they interpreted moving on. Moving forward is a continuation of life with the past intact, while moving on has more of a sense of forgetting the past. With this in mind, it is no wonder that my kids were opposed to having me date. With my new understanding, I decided that I would date even though it was against my kids' discretion. I figured that they would forgive me someday. And they have.

As Jen mentioned, I had planned to pick up my daughter Noel from college. It was December of 2017, and she was coming home for Christmas break. I told my other two kids that I would be leaving a couple of days early to meet Jen. I wanted to see her as much as possible before taking Noel home to California. Jen and I had already established a bond by chatting online, texting, and talking on the phone. But meeting each other made me nervous. The night before I'd planned to leave for Utah, I couldn't sleep, so I got up at 3:30 a.m. I packed up the car and left. About two hours into my drive after driving through the Sierra mountains, I needed to stop and rest in Reno for a couple of hours. Before I got back on the road, I drank a couple of highly caffeinated drinks for energy. My body was not used to large amounts of caffeine, so my hands were shaky and my body was jittery. My lack of sleep also made me feel weak. But I continued on because Jen and I were going to meet at a particular place and at a particular time in Utah. I was getting impatient in my drive through Nevada so I began driving faster even though I had plenty of time to get there. Then it happened!

In what has become my custom, I got a speeding ticket just outside of Elko, Nevada. When I was pulled over, the highway patrol officer asked if I knew how fast I was driving.

I said, "I was driving eighty-nine miles per hour."

"That's right!" the officer said. "Thank you for being honest."

The officer then took my driver's license back to his squad car to scan. It took him a considerable amount of time to come back to my car. Before he did, another patrol car arrived. This other officer came to the side of my car and asked how I was doing. I told him I was fine, and that I was just a little tired.

The officer pointed to my hands and said, "Your hands are pretty shaky."

"Yes," I said, "I've had a little too much caffeine."

"Okay," he said. "Be safe out there."

I quickly realized that the second officer was called because they thought perhaps I was on drugs because of my shaking hands. The two officers deliberated for a few minutes until the first officer came back to my car.

He said, "I gave you a ticket in this same place for driving eighty-nine miles per hour last year."

I replied, "Yes, I think I remember that."

"Well," he said, "since you were honest about your speed, I'm going to write you up as going seventy-five miles per hour so that you'll have to pay less money for the ticket."

"Thank you," I said.

He then warned me, "If I meet you again in the future, I won't be so nice."

"Okay," I said. "I'll slow it down."

The officer had me sign the ticket and gave me a copy. When I got back on the road I drove slowly until both highway patrol vehicles were no longer behind me. Within a few hours, I made it to Utah.

I drove all the way to Station Park, an outdoor shopping mall in Farmington, Utah. This was where Jen and I had planned to meet. I was so excited to meet her. I perused the area and saw a lot of people with blonde hair, but I couldn't find her. I was still a bit early, so I called her to find out where she was. She said she was about forty-five minutes away. I was surprised. It was 4:50 and we had planned to meet at 5:00. I had been in the car for over twelve hours, and she was running late on her forty-five-minute drive. Thoughts began to cross my mind: "Was she really planning on meeting me? Did I get stood up?" I was relieved when Jen suggested that we meet someplace between Farmington and South Jordan. The obvious answer was Temple Square, in Salt Lake City.

The First Date, a Prelude to Dating

Jen

When I arrived at Temple Square, I remember having so many emotions swirling around in my mind and in my heart. I'd arrived first and waited near the Christmas nativity scene. When Justin finally approached me, I felt speechless. We embraced for a long time, and I put both hands on his cheeks to make sure he was real. We spent the evening getting to know each other face-to-face. The reality of who a person is cannot be realized through social media, texting, or over the phone. You have to be face-to-face, and we were for the entire night. The conversations were effortless, and he made me feel comfortable. The ease of familiarity caught me by surprise. Was I really with a man who was interested in more than just hearing me tell all the details of my story? One who had a mutual understanding about the difficulty of losing a spouse? Who understood what it's like to be an only parent? The answer to all of these questions was simply "Yes!"

Justin

U pon first seeing Jen, I thought she was beautiful. I had seen pictures of her but nothing compared to real life. As I approached her she could see that I was still shaking from the large amounts of caffeine in my system and she thought it was a bad sign. She thought it meant that I was disappointed. But I was far from it. She said, "Oh no!" I was taken back a bit. But the look in her eyes exuded caring. I assured her that I was not disappointed in meeting her. When we hugged for the first time, there was nothing strange about it. I was prepared to show affection because I'd prepared myself to start dating. I felt no guilt, no need to keep myself in check, no need to keep my guard up. Adult dating is all about timing. Dating has little to do with the amount of time one has been widowed and a lot to do with listening to your heart, listening to your mind, and for some, it has to do with listening to your children.

We had a lovely first date that none of our kids would have approved of. When a person becomes widowed and has teenage children, a bilateral relationship develops in the home. In the case with my kids, I was their dad, and they were my mom. Thus, in Jen's house, she was their mom, and her kids were her dad. It's a peculiar dynamic—the role that children try to take on when they lose a parent. They may take on a parent-like role when they talk to you. But I'm convinced through my own experience that they're just protective—they don't want you to get hurt in any way. They may take on a parental tone because they care about you and haven't yet learned how to approach certain situations that may cause them anxiety. They need only be reminded that you are the parent and they are still your children. This will bring the respect back that they might not have shown if they've acted bossy. Remember that the situation in losing a parent is very traumatic for children of any age. They've seen firsthand that their parents are not invincible. They'll trust you when you redraw the boundaries. But it could take some time.

Showing Your Scars

Perhaps the most important thing that Jen and I did early on in our relationship was something that I call "showing your scars." Our desires were to be totally transparent and inform each other of our personal struggles and issues that had become triumphs. I knew that honesty was the most important aspect of our relationship, as indeed it should be for everyone. I wanted to give Jen the details of who I was to alleviate her fear of the unknown. I wanted to know the details of who Jen was, so that I could also make an informed decision about the direction that our relationship should go.

We knew that being strong in the passing of our spouses didn't necessarily mean that we could endure any type of hardship that life could throw at us. We thought just the opposite. We didn't want to be hurt again. We didn't want any bombs going off, so to speak, that would broadside one another and cause problems that we had never anticipated as our relationship grew. Showing our scars was a defensive strategy that we both took on to truly get to know each other deeply and quickly.

We shared things that we thought could potentially affect our relationship in the future so that we'd have time to process the hard things that each of us would inherit by being together. We were honest and open with each other. We wanted to learn what issues we were each harboring from our real-life experiences that could potentially bring our relationship to a halt.

In a way it was like saying, "This is why I think you probably won't want to be with me." Or, "These are my issues, do you think you could handle them." It sounds strange for two people who already cared so much for each other to be exchanging "why nots," but it was an effective way to scaffold a relationship of truth by breaking through any pretentiousness or dishonesty. If our relationship was going to end based on information that might break us up, we felt the sooner the better. Jen and I wanted to know the dirt in the details of our lives so we could decide if our relationship was worth making the sacrifices that it would take to continue moving forward.

Jen explained that she had serious trust issues that stemmed from her first marriage and the tragic way that things ended. She asked me very pointed questions about morality and faithfulness. For example, the first question she asked was if I looked at pornography. That was a fair question, and it deserved an honest answer. My answer was, "No." She continued to explain the nature of her trust issues, how they came to be, as well as what she would and wouldn't tolerate in a relationship.

Then it was my turn. I asked Jen what her understanding was of bipolar disorder. As it turned out, she knew what it was; however, I knew that I needed to explain to her that it could disrupt the lives of others as much as it can disrupt the person living with the illness. I proceeded by saying that it could drastically complicate relationships in marriage and in daily living. I assured her as honestly as I could that I have taken medications for years and that I tried to maintain a lifestyle that helped me manage the illness. I told her frankly that the illness was there and that it was a strain on my first marriage at times when I was sick and out of work. I wanted her to know that it would be possible for me to experience a mania or fall into depression even if I was taking my medications. I knew that she was a member of a Facebook closed group that dealt with complicated grief and that some widows on that site had lost their bipolar spouse to suicide. The statistics for bipolar type 1 are astounding in that approximately 15 percent die by suicide ("Bipolar Disorder and Self-Injury," WebMD). She had lost her husband to suicide. So, naturally, she needed to know that although I'd never had those tendencies, numbers were numbers and she'd have to trust that it would never ever be an option for me. It just isn't in my nature.

I could see that Jen felt that she needed more than just my word that I was who I said I was. So I offered to call a friend in the Relief Society Presidency in California. I dialed the number and said, "Hi, Lisa, I'm here with Jen, the widow in Utah that I told you about. Would you be willing to talk to her about my character? And about what kind of person I am?"

Lisa said, "I'd be happy to. Is she there now?"

"Yes," I answered.

"Okay," she said. "Put her on the phone."

This may have been an unorthodox way of easing Jen's concerns, but it was the right thing to do at the moment. As Jen talked to Lisa, I walked into another room feeling confident that Lisa would vouch for me. She was in fact a neighbor, a fellow churchgoer, and a family friend. But I didn't want to speculate about what was being said, so I just kept a positive mindset as I listened to the muffled sounds of Jen's voice in the other room as she asked questions about me.

Every widow and widower has difficulties, fears, and emotional scars to one degree or another. It seems to go with the territory. This is not to assume that we are all wounded beyond repair. It just means that we're healing from the difficulties that we've been faced with. The benefit of having hard discussions early on in our dating experience was that we were able to talk through our struggles honestly and to analyze them together.

For me, being in a relationship with somebody who lived 637 miles away gave me the desire to maximize our time together. After all, precious children were also to be involved should we happen to get married. Talking through the complications early on helped create an atmosphere that was open and honest from the start. Neither of us wanted to hold a weight of confusion or lack of awareness as our relationship progressed. We soon found out that we didn't have to.

Considerations

♡ What will you tell your children when you decide that you're ready to date? Are you prepared for their reactions?

♡ Would it be best to tell your children that you are seeing somebody as just a friend or that you have a romantic involvement? Perhaps it depends on where your relationship stands.

♡ Would you feel comfortable introducing the person that you are dating to your children? When you're in a committed relationship with somebody, it will need to happen sooner or later.

CHAPTER 7

What Other People Say About Dating

True love requires action.

—*Elder Dieter F. Uchtdorf*

What Will People Say?

Jen

The connection between Justin and I was instant, and the Spirit confirmed that it was right. It was exciting, and I was surprised that my heart could feel what it was feeling. Love. And so soon! But despite my enthusiasm about him, I was hesitant to tell people. Not because I wasn't feeling positive about where things were going, but because I knew that opinions and advice would start pouring in.

Two months before my husband's suicide, my mom had passed away. She'd suffered many health problems with her heart along with diabetes for many years, and in December 2015 she died. My mom was my best friend. I was still in the very early stages of bereavement from her death when Stoney took his life. I ached to have her here on earth with me. I felt empty without her comfort. My dad, at age seventy-seven, and I, at age forty, had both become widowed. I add this detail because being widowed is indeed tragic whether you are in the very early stages of marriage or you've been married for many years. And those who love you want to protect you from being hurt, which can happen when the dating process begins.

However, friends, family members, and my priesthood leaders were cautiously supportive. They knew the hurt I'd been through and did not want to see me rush into something prematurely. I completely understood this perspective. If I were in their shoes looking at me, I might have offered the same advice.

Here is my advice: if you do decide to open your heart and love again, stay true to yourself. When people learned that I was dating again, some of the responses I got were, "Well, that's so nice you've made a friend. You need others that understand you." But it was more than that. We were in love and we knew it. While I did receive some very good counsel, we knew the direction we were headed. When either of us received words of warning, it was sometimes discouraging, but we knew we were the ones who were going to make the decisions. No one knows how the next chapter of your life will begin except you. After all, it's your life. We both felt strongly throughout our seven months of dating that we wanted to keep moving forward as we saw fit. We did it for us!

Justin

There is a lot to be said about dating after being widowed—so much that I could write volumes about it and share the diversification of opinions that I got from every direction imaginable. In short, everyone who loves you, everyone who knows you, everyone who knows your story, anyone who is a mere acquaintance, and anyone who feels like they're in any way a part of your life, will want to hear details and give you advice about dating. It's up to you to decide what to do with the reactions of others. Will you let the reactions of others dictate how you handle your relationship? Will you take their opinions to heart? Whose counsel will you trust the most? Who will you turn to for advice?

Unfortunately, there is no success formula for deciding when to date, who to date, or how to avoid a person that if you had all the facts, you might never want to date. As mentioned before, some widows and widowers may struggle to know when the timing is right, while others may unquestionably know exactly when and who they want to share a romantic relationship with. Remember that ultimately the decisions that you'll have to live with are the decisions that you make. You'll definitely receive advice, whether it's solicited or not, but it's important to use your own best judgment in your dating decisions. And of course, always take it to the Lord for discernment.

Beware of anyone who cites statistics about how many second marriages end in divorce. It can be rather discouraging. Throughout the time that Jen and I were dating, we were informed numerous times by numerous people that the statistics of successful second marriages are quite low, with a large percentage of remarried couples ending up in divorce. I was told on several occasions that up to 75 percent of second marriages fail. However, in my research, I have found no solid data to support such broad claims.

In my view, it is certain that the numbers and figures are largely irrelevant because of the many considerations that are omitted no matter how comprehensive the research seems to be. With all things considered, the statistics will never match up with reality regardless of the sources. The evidence is too thin. Although the percentage of failed second marriages has been shown to be higher than for first marriages, truthfully, what do people expect you to do—not get married again? I was a widower. The "traditional family" part of my life had already happened. I was no longer a part of the club. I was without the partner that I had planned to spend the rest of my life with.

I was told by several people that we should wait until all of our children were ready for us to get married. This advice invited the question, "Is it wrong to fall in love with someone if your kids think it's not the right time, or if they think that it's wrong altogether?" My response to questions like this invoked another question, "Does anyone really believe that seven children are going to be on the same page about remarriage and blending families after they've lost a parent?" Furthermore, I didn't believe that our kids would ever get together and in unison say, "Just do it! We want you to remarry as soon as possible." If we had chosen to wait until all our kids were comfortable with our decision, I don't know if our remarriage would have ever happened. Marriage is a sensitive topic. When you have children, your decision will affect everyone. Not everyone has to be on board at every step but it's sure nice to have the support of your children. That should be the goal. Having your children's support. It will make blending so much simpler when you get there. However, children have their agency to decide if or when to support your decision.

Meeting the Family

Jen

When the time came for Justin to meet my dad and my brothers, I informed him of the jokes that my dad would tell during lunch, and sure enough, he told the jokes that I expected him to tell. This made it easy for Justin to understand when to laugh agreeably. The meeting was lighthearted but serious. My favorite memory of our lunch together was when my brother Gail broke in and stopped our conversation to ask Justin a question.

"What are your intentions with my sister?"

We all laughed and started talking again. But my brother stopped and asked the question again.

"Seriously, though, what are your intentions with my sister?"

Justin realized that he couldn't evade the question.

He said, "I'm very fond of her. I want to get to know her better and see where our relationship takes us."

My brother replied, "Okay, but if you hurt her, I'll have to find a place to dispose of your body."

Smiling, Justin said, "Okay, I don't want to disappoint her, and I don't want to upset a man of your stature."

Although it was a light moment, my brother made me feel loved and cared for.

Justin

On my second trip to Utah, my parents happened to be in town visiting my sisters. I arranged a lunch date for them to meet Jen. Because they lived in California at the time, they had heard me talk about Jen's great qualities, but they had no idea who it really was that I was talking about. I wanted them to know the person that I was falling in love with. I wanted to know what they thought of her.

We had a nice lunch together breaking the ice. My dad was quiet and observant as Jen and my mom conversed nearly the entire time. As we were leaving, my mom embraced Jen and started to cry.

I heard her say, "I just want Justin to be happy."

It warmed my heart to hear my mother's words, and to me, it meant her approval. It was a priceless moment.

A Meaningful Exchange

A couple of years ago, as I was preparing to speak at a Widows/Widowers Conference about blending families, I requested an interview with my brother-in-law Jasen to discuss widowhood. Jasen is not a widower. He and my sister Alisa have been married for ten years and had for a long time been unable to conceive. But in 2016, they were blessed with a miracle child by the process of in vitro fertilization. From the time that their daughter Sydney was born, Jasen and Alisa have cherished every moment they've had with her. Knowing Jasen to be a loving husband and father, I hoped he would have rich insight as to what he would do if Alisa passed away, leaving him to raise Sydney alone.

I prefaced the interview with a request that he wouldn't answer any of my questions with the simple responses that widows and widowers most commonly get. The ground rules were that he couldn't start any of his comments with the following phrases: "I can't imagine . . . ," "I can only imagine . . . ," "I don't know how . . . ," and "I could never . . ." Personally, I could never have imagined being widowed at age forty-one, but it happened. I had never thought about the what-ifs until my late wife passed away.

My hopes were that Jasen would be willing to internalize some difficult questions and to speak about the unlikely prospect of losing my sister at a young age. Jasen listened intently to my questions, and I had a pen and paper ready to write down his answers. Admittedly, the questions I asked were extremely difficult to answer if you'd never lost a spouse.

I began: "How would you feel if Alisa passed away today, and what would you do to move forward in life?"

After a great deal of thought, Jasen began, "Losing Alisa would be devastating. So much of my thinking and consideration is directed toward her every day. The most important part of our family would be missing." He continued, "I would feel so much emptiness in life if she were gone."

I wrote down his response and then asked: "How would you feel about continuing to work and leaving Sydney to be cared for by someone else if you couldn't be there yourself?"

He replied, "I guess it would depend on Sydney's age, but I'd definitely need the help of family."

I continued: "Whether you'd remarry or not, would you ever feel like you had a normal family again?"

"That's a good question," he began. "Heavenly Father wants us to have families, and they're not all put together in the same way. He blesses us without regard to our perception of what an ideal family looks like to us."

Jasen further explained that if we follow the Spirit's guidance, the Lord will have a hand in our family lives.

He then said, "Anything that Heavenly Father has a hand in is a good thing. Every family is different, and every family can love each other and work through challenges together."

I then asked him: "What would you do to comfort and nurture Sydney if you were in the midst of the grieving process yourself?"

He again said that caring for Sydney would depend on her age, and also how well she could understand the permanence of losing a parent. Jasen articulated that he would have the humility to request help from family in taking care of Sydney, which would bring him comfort in knowing that she was in caring hands.

It became obvious to me that Jasen had heeded the counsel that we have received from modern prophets and apostles to take the time to discuss and prepare temporally for tough things that might be on the horizon. As our interview concluded, I thanked Jasen for the time he took to talk about things that we don't generally want to think or talk about. Preparedness for unlikely events is so important. However, there is a stark difference between healthy *consideration* of events that *could* happen in our lives and deep *comprehension* of events that *have* happened in our lives. There are things that we just can't prepare enough for, and that's exactly where the Lord comes in to pick up the slack.

Considerations

♡ Are you prepared to receive counsel and advice from others about dating? How will you respond to it? Who will you listen to?

♡ Be mindful of difficult decisions that must be made every step of the way in courtship. The margin for error is slim, and the potential ramifications are many. Who all will be affected by your decisions?

♡ Remember that nobody has or can walk even the shortest of steps in your shoes. Discouragement is always permitted, but so is encouragement. Take what you will to heart, and take it to the Lord.

CHAPTER 8

Pitfalls and Pit Stops: Introducing the Children

To Him, our direction is more important than our speed.
—*Larry R. Lawrence*

A *pit stop* is defined as a temporary deviation from a direct course. A *pitfall* is defined as a difficulty that is not easily recognized. (Merriam-Webster) Amidst the progress of any romantic relationship, there will always be *pit stops* and *pitfalls* that may require you to readdress, reconsider, or reaffirm your commitment to the person you are dating. My children wanted to know who I was dating, if it was exclusive, and how serious my relationship was. It's safe to assume that children will always want to have a say in who you are dating and whether or not it's the right time for them to accept that a parent's relationship is moving from casual to serious.

Shortly after Jen and I started dating, our children began assuming that more changes were coming, and rightly so. Opposition came in waves, and sometimes it was one crest after another. My kids would see me staring at my phone smiling as I read texts from Jen, and then they'd watch me immediately reply with a sense of vigor that they had never seen before. It was foreign to them, and they didn't like it.

What an odd thing it must be for kids to see their widowed parent flirt with another person for the first time. Whenever I was confronted by my kids, I would explain that I needed a friend and it was my right to have one. They would instinctively say, "You've got us!" Children don't want their widowed parent to be unhappy and feel isolated. They want us to be happy. But sometimes they just want us to be happy on their terms.

Adult to adult interaction is healthy and important. Perhaps children realize this. But when you begin to develop strong feelings for a person who isn't their parent, it's likely that they will feel uncomfortable with it. However, as was stated in the previous chapter, whether or not your children are ready for you to press forward, it's your call. This might sound insensitive, but it's a decision that is the parent's right to make. If changes are coming, parents get to call the shots. We should be prayerful and know for certainty that the Lord knows what's best for us and our families. Pit stops and pitfalls may abound, yet they can be taken in stride. If it's not the right time now, it doesn't mean that it will *never* be the right time.

A potential pit stop could be that the kids raise havoc, so you decide to give your relationship a rest for a time. A pitfall could be that your collective kids may not like each other upon meeting, so maybe you give it a rest for a longer period of time. But sooner or later you might have to put your foot down and say, "Hey! I deserve to have a personal life just like everyone else in the family. And I deserve to have companionship just as you will someday."

Introducing the Children

As Spring was approaching, we wanted our children to meet each other. But they were all in school, so it wasn't possible for them to meet in person yet. We went with the assumption that the use of simple technology would break down barriers that our children were putting up, and it did! On a particular Sunday, we decided to do a family FaceTime. Who doesn't like to FaceTime? It turned out to be a great icebreaker. A seed of familiarity was planted, and soon FaceTiming families became a regular Sunday night activity. It lightened my heart to hear our children interact.

Also, Grant created a family Snapchat and called it "The Ellertons," referring to the Ellers and the Wintertons. The kids had a lot of fun sending Snapchat photos to each other with comments about how things were going in their lives. They also enjoyed sending pictures of our two grief dogs, Coda and Bella. Now, over three years later, the Ellerton Snapchat is alive and well. It's a mode of communication that we all enjoy.

The Adventure Begins

During spring break of 2017, Jen and I were determined to get the kids to meet and get to know each other in person prior to our getting engaged to be married. Jen brought three of her kids out to California. Our hope was that we would witness some cohesiveness between our children. I'd met Jen's kids on my first two trips to Utah, and she had met my kids on a trip to California. But this time it was family to family. The potential pitfalls that we'd heard about stepsiblings being at odds with each other was a worry at first. And it was a worry that resurfaced every now and then for the entire time that we were dating. We'd heard that it could become a nightmare, but we knew that it was equally possible that they would be friendly toward each other.

Fortunately, my oldest daughter, Noel, was home from BYUI for the quarter. Unfortunately, Jen's oldest daughter, Marie, was in Europe on a study abroad through BYU, but she would soon catch up on her own trip to California later. All of our kids needed to meet each other so we found ways to make it happen.

Despite Noel's initial disapproval of how quickly things were moving in my relationship with Jen, she planned a trip to Santa Cruz for a day, and we were happy to follow her plan. Noel and I rode together in her car. We needed some father-daughter time to catch up on where things stood in her life as a college student. We took the lead as Jen followed us in her car with the other five children. "Poor Jen," I thought to myself. "She's outnumbered by the kids five to one." I was interested in hearing what Noel's opinion was of me furthering my relationship, and I wanted to know how she felt about Jen's kids. She voluntarily gave her approval of Jen and her children as she said, "I have to admit, Jen's kids are cooler than I thought they would be." I greatly appreciated her opinion, as I was seeking her approval partially because she is my oldest child and completely because she was the most skeptical of my three children.

Also on my agenda was to talk to Noel about an unhealthy relationship that she was in at BYUI. I wanted our talk to be private and personal. What a strange dilemma for a forty-three-year-old father to be in! I'd never imagined that I would one day be in a mutual conversation with one of my children about who we were dating. It felt as if I were walking a tightrope a mile high to be seeking my daughter's approval and getting it while I was preparing to reasonably disapprove of a relationship that she was in. I approached the topic carefully. I didn't want any hurt feelings or receive backlash by being too blunt. With caution, I alluded to the fact that her boyfriend was not good enough for her. And I left it at that for the time being. I didn't want to erase her support of my relationship with Jen.

The day in Santa Cruz was a success. Everyone enjoyed the beach, the boardwalk, shopping, playing games, and going on rides. At times, I still look at the pictures we took together that day, and I feel like it was a miraculous experience seeing the kids enjoying their time together as we witnessed them bonding for the first time. There was no awkwardness, and to my relief, they all wanted to get to know each other better. It was a day full of precious moments.

At dusk, we began to venture home. Noel and I rode together again, but we accidentally ditched Jen on the winding road from Santa Cruz to San Jose. Noel and I gave no consideration to the fact that for Jen it was an unfamiliar drive back to Lincoln. As I sat in the passenger seat of Noel's car, Grant called me three times asking where we were, as they were trying to follow us on the winding pass through the hills.

As Noel and I made it to our predetermined pit stop, we pulled into the gas station. I was on the phone again with Grant as it became obvious that they had lost their way. I knew that Jen's car was lagging behind us somewhere.

My answer to Grant was the same as the first three times he called, "We're just ahead of you, stay on the highway and you'll be fine."

The fourth time that Grant called me, I told him that we had stopped at our specified pit stop to get gas.

Grant's answer was, "We already went off the highway!"

I heard laughing and crying in the background. Jen had apparently taken the wrong exit. In the darkness, she hit a bush and narrowly missed some orange barrels along the off-ramp. I didn't know the details at the time or I would have taken what he was telling me much more seriously.

I asked, "Where are you guys now?"

Grant replied, "I'm not sure. We're in the parking lot of a motel with a flickering vacancy sign. It looks scary."

I started laughing. I thought it was a joke, so I put Grant on speakerphone and asked him to tell the story again so that Noel and I could hear what happened and share a laugh. I would soon find out that it wasn't a joke. Jen really had hit a bush and narrowly missed the orange barrels when she exited off the freeway. And they really did end up in the parking lot of a cheap motel that had a flickering vacancy sign. It was a pitfall that could have ended really badly. Fortunately, no one was hurt. Needless to say, we finally found each other, and our caravan made it home safely. Jen and I were so pleased that we'd had a peaceful, fun time together. It was a further witness to us that what we were doing was right.

Considerations

♡ In what ways can you prepare your children to meet each other?

♡ Have you considered that the age of your children could dictate their outlook about meeting someone else's children? The reactions of young children can be much different than the reactions of teenagers and young adults.

♡ Is there an exciting way to introduce each other's children that they will respond to? The use of technology can make for a nonthreatening way for kids to interact.

CHAPTER 9

Facing the Big Decisions

For last year's words belong to last year's language
And next year's words await another voice.

—*T. S. Eliot, "Little Gidding"*

I felt great apprehension in telling my children that I was going to ask Jen to marry me. Not only were they going to experience living as a new family unit, but I had also decided that my little family was going to move from California to Jen's home turf in Utah. Getting remarried sometimes requires one or both families to uproot and move to an unfamiliar place. Such was the case with us. It took me several months of prayer and contemplation about how to approach my children and tell them that I planned on getting engaged to Jen. It was a double-edged sword. If my children knew that Jen and I were going to be married, they also knew that we would be moving across state lines.

I rehearsed the ways and means of discussing engagement without breaking their hearts. Telling them that they were going to have to leave their friends who had comforted them through so many hard times, friends they had grown up with, and all the familiarities of the place we'd called home for a large portion of their lives was one of the most difficult things that I've ever had to address. My heart ached for them. It was the kind of heartache that runs through the entire body.

I didn't want there to be any unnecessary hardship to prevail in our planned move. I prayed that they would somehow be prepared for the fear of the unknown that they would inevitably feel, as it would require another major adjustment that they'd have to make after the hard times they'd already gone through in losing their mother. I knew I would have to be patient with them, and I was. But I told them that, as the patriarch of the home, it was up to me to lead them into doing what was right for all of us. I told them to pray for a witness of their own to know that it was right and good and true. I paced myself in how quickly I asked for their full support and tried to be patient with them. I knew that if I could receive answers from the Lord, they could too. I prayed often that they would receive answers for themselves.

Jen

A Planned Proposal

In June 2017, after we had been dating for six months, Justin arranged for a trip to Utah in which I expected that he was going to propose to me. After all, we had already decided to get married, but with him teaching until the end of the school year, June was the earliest he could fly out. I had already been actively coordinating our wedding that would take place in July.

When Justin arrived, we planned to go out on a Saturday night, but he wouldn't tell me where we were going. He drove me to a place with a view of the valley. It was a place that we'd often gone to talk. He asked me to explain three reasons why I would want to marry him. Then, he reciprocated with three of his own reasons that he would want to marry me.

I didn't know where else we would be going, but shortly after he began driving again, he quickly pulled over and said, "Oh no!"

"What?" I asked.

"We've got to head back to the house! I've forgotten something," he replied.

So we turned around and drove back to the house. I laughed inside, thinking he'd forgotten to bring the engagement ring with him.

I was going to wait in the car, but he turned it off, walked over to my side, and opened the door. He told me I should come into the house because it was going to take a few minutes. When we got to the front door, it opened. My youngest daughter Kate was dressed in a dress and apron.

She said, "Welcome to the Haven House. Will there be two of you this evening?"

Justin said, "Ah yes, we have a reservation for two."

As we walked into the house, what I saw was breathtaking. Kate directed us to our dining room table, which had been set for dinner by candlelight. We were given beautifully hand-drawn menus as we were seated. Soon Grant appeared and poured us each a drink of sparkling apple cider. Then, Colby brought us some warm bread with butter. Both boys were wearing T-shirts with bow ties.

This was our destination for the night. Our home. The children had turned our dining room into a fine restaurant. It was precious beyond words. Ashlee appeared from the kitchen wearing a dress and explained that she was the restaurant manager and that she hoped we would enjoy our dinner. There was only one choice on the menu, so Justin and I ordered the same thing: chicken, rice, and a side salad. Ashlee wrote our orders on a small notepad and walked back to the kitchen, where the food was being prepared. Everything was set up beautifully. Soon dinner was served by our two boys.

As we were eating, Justin asked, "Jen, do you think we can do this?"

He didn't specify what "this" meant. But I knew that he was referring to "us." Our future together, with all seven of our children.

"Yes," I answered, "I know we can."

"Good," he said. "So do I."

"How is your food?" he asked me with a smile on his face.

"It's delicious," I replied.

"Would you like some dessert?"

"Sure," I answered.

Justin tapped on his cider glass, and Ashlee came out from the kitchen. He ordered the only dessert listed on the menu: a mixed bowl of Ghirardelli's individually wrapped chocolates. While Ashlee brought our dessert, I could see Grant from the corner of my eye. He was setting up a camera phone so that our children who weren't there would have a chance to see what transpired.

When Ashlee brought us the bowl of chocolates, I could see several of our kids anxiously watching us from the kitchen. It was a heartwarming sight. Justin began digging through the chocolates, picking out my favorite kinds, and putting them on a small plate in front of me. Amid the pile of chocolates was a velvet ring case. He pulled the case from the pile of chocolates, got down on one knee, and held it in front of me. I was expecting to hear the words, "Will you . . ." But I didn't. And he hadn't opened the case to reveal what was inside. There was a long pause as he looked into my eyes.

He then asked, "Who do you think will win the World Series this year, Jen?"

A bit panicky, I said, "The Yankees."

He then opened the case, and it was empty. I was a little confused as he said, "No, Jen, the Giants are going to win the World Series."

"Um, okay," I replied.

"But baseball isn't everything. Will you marry me?" he asked as he pulled a beautiful diamond ring from his pocket.

"Yes!" I said.

He then slipped the ring on my finger, and we kissed and hugged for a very, very, long time. At this point, the kids came running into the dining room, and we all began to hug each other. It was a moment of joy—it was as if the anguish that was brought upon both of our families was peeled back long enough for us to feel the happiness of what would soon become a new beginning.

As I was in Justin's arms, thoughts came into my mind. They were vivid memories of my mom who had passed away just eighteen months before. I could feel that her joy and excitement matched my own. I felt her approval. I felt her love. I felt that everything was right.

We're Engaged; Let the Work Begin

Jen

When you've been extremely traumatized by the sudden loss of a parent, it's human nature to try to control anything and everything you can in the past, present, and future. The children probably knew that Justin and I were going to get engaged to be married as quickly as we realized it ourselves. And within months of our meeting, it did happen. I remember one exchange I had with Marie after Justin and I were engaged. On one particular day, she was very emotional and worried about the upcoming wedding, which was just about a month away. She felt unsettled about it. Many questions swirled around in her mind, and it was overwhelming her. Just a few months prior she had received a mission call to serve in Arizona Scottsdale Mission, Spanish speaking. She would be leaving for her mission just three weeks after our upcoming wedding. Needless to say, there was a storm of feelings in her heart and mind. She's the oldest of my children and has always been what I call "an old and wise soul." She's intuitive and nurturing and likes to take charge. I tried to calm her anxieties by sharing with her the spiritual confirmation I had received about marrying Justin and joining our families. I shared with her that I knew it was right. I told her that I knew the Lord was happy with this decision.

I expected that after really testifying this to her, what I was saying would instantaneously feel true to her heart too. But she said, "Well that's great for you, Mom. I'm glad you've received that answer. But I haven't received it yet! That's not how I feel!" I told her that was okay. I asked her to continue to seek an answer in prayer and, for a time, to lean on my conviction—to lean on my faith and to have hope for a bright future.

Another way to assure children is to express what their deceased parent must be feeling! That they are so grateful that the spouse they left behind is finding happiness and that they want their children to be happy and taken care of. Their parent that has passed through the veil is still their parent. And they will continually be a part of their lives. A new parental figure is in no way a replacement, but an additional person who loves them very much.

Through the Holy Ghost, our Heavenly Father confirms the truth of all things. He's told us that in the scriptures many times. And especially in times when we are leery or nervous about anything, including a family change that is going to take place. Both personal and family prayer can be the key.

Lastly, it's important to remember that even when we've had a witness from the Holy Ghost that something is true, we may still at times question it. We may still question previous convictions with the onset of every-day struggles or nuances that may cause us to question ourselves. These uncertainties can be frequent in the beginning while adjustments take place in uniting two families. Just because the Spirit has once confirmed that a decision is right, it does NOT mean that there will not be highs and lows—good days and bad days.

Remind your children to ask the Lord to give them peace that the prayers that have already been answered are true. And that the questions they are still seeking answers to will be answered in time. It's okay for every-one to be on a different page in receiving conviction. Justin and I have always agreed that it's important that we are open with the kids and that they can express how they feel about being a part of our blended family.

Justin

After getting engaged, Jen and I decided it was never too early to start planning our lives together. So we began looking for answers to two fundamental questions that we had. The first and obvious question was, "How can we best make a marriage work after widowhood?" The second question we had was, "How can we successfully blend families with children who have suffered from the grief and trauma of losing a parent?"

As one might presume, our two fundamental questions could invoke answers branching out into the infinities. But we wanted to hear from the experts. And I don't mean family therapists. We had a threefold qualification for individuals or couples before we would ask them for any advice. Was at least one of them widowed? Were they remarried? Were they blending families? In addition to this, Jen and I looked for books about blending families at bookstores and found that most of them don't carry that many books in stock on any of these topics. So our answers had to come from friends that we knew were blending.

We already understood that with any well-functioning family the marriage comes first—it must be a healthy relationship even if it's a second or third marriage. Jen and I wanted to learn as much as we could about husbands and wives working together in addressing children/stepchildren and parent/stepparent relationships. We took into account that the crucial planning time that young couples have in their first marriages was largely irrelevant to our situation because the challenges of blending children and stepchildren begin immediately after the wedding is over. That makes for a short honeymoon period. Many of the new realities were new to us, and we didn't feel like we were capable of fully understanding the difficulties that could arise without talking to people who had been there, and who were still there.

We decided to interview willing couples who were in the position that we'd soon be in. They turned out to be the experts—those couples who had been in our situation and were living it every day. We sought opportunities to speak with people who were immersed in the process of creating a "new normal" for their families. I remember several occasions when we communicated by FaceTime with couples who we couldn't visit with in person, asking questions and taking notes. We would write down questions in advance and discuss them.

The first questions on our agenda were about marriage. We asked many questions about people's experiences and the challenges of remarriage after being widowed. Some of which had to do with personal matters like having alone time to strengthen the marriage, showing appropriate affection, intimacy, modeling a healthy marriage, and developing a new lifestyle together. After discussing the important components of remarriage, we began with the blending questions.

- We asked about the easy and the hard parts of uniting two sets of children.

- We asked about specific challenges that couples were facing with regard to their children's relationships with each other.

- We asked couples what they did about living arrangements due to their children's ages and genders.

- We asked if they recommended buying a new house or moving into a house that was owned by one or the other.

- We asked about daily challenges that blended families were facing.
- We asked if any of their children were having trouble bonding in their stepchild and stepparent relationships.
- We asked about the difficulties in developing new family routines.
- We asked for advice about disciplining children in a blended family.

This was a notable way to learn about blending families. The information that we gathered was most relevant to us because it came from those who had personal experience in these areas. By hearing real-life experiences of couples blending families, we gained valuable insight on where to start and what to anticipate in moving forward.

Considerations

♡ If you plan on getting married, children must be prepared to face the prospect of engagement and what it entails. How can you prepare your children to hear about your plans and what will you do to gain their support?

♡ Do you feel it's necessary to have every child's support before you get engaged? How will you respond if you don't have full support?

♡ Is there a way to have your children be a part of your engagement experience? This can be highly beneficial for everybody.

CHAPTER 10

The Strength of Commitment

True love is not something you fall in, but grow in.

—*Lynn G. Robbins*

Our Commitment to Each Other

Jen

Before we got to the point of getting remarried, we as parents had to have a commitment between us that we were going to make it work. If you picture a pyramid, it must be built from the foundation up. We had to establish a strong foundation in our relationship first and foremost, and we had to build true devotion to each other. Our relationship had to be first on the list in order to have the strength to build on the rest of the family structure. We had to be getting married for the right reasons, not because we happened to be widowed, or for financial purposes, or that my kids needed a dad and that Justin's kids needed a mom. None of these things would matter if we didn't answer the most important questions first: Do I love this person? Do I want to be with this person for the rest of my life? Do I get along with this person? Do we love to be together? Are we willing to make a commitment that our relationship comes first? Do we have all the things that we had going into our first marriage, or even more?

You must go into marriage after being widowed with just as much commitment as you had in your first marriage. Also, you must be consciously aware that there are the added challenges of having grieving children in a new family, all of whom have separate and distinct personalities. You must be solid as a couple to be able to meet the demands of creating a blended family successfully.

Second marriages need to be built on sturdy ground. This is essential because it creates security and reassurance to children who desperately need stability in the home. The devotion that we bring to a second marriage cannot be based on the logistics of it. It has to be for love. And it has to be what you know is right, and you must be loyal to it. You have to be willing to work together through hard things because hard things sit on your doorstep. Once you make the decision to blend, the difficulties won't wait to be invited in.

The difficulty begins on day one. You have to be willing to work hard together all day, every day. In a first marriage, you tell your children, "Dad and Mom's relationship comes first." In a second marriage, children need to have the same reminders: "Our marriage comes first, and having you taken care of is absolutely essential, but I'm not going to be disloyal to my husband/ wife." The substance of the marriage must be strong or it becomes like an upside-down triangle with no foundation to build upon.

The points that I would like to summarize are these: The kids WILL have opposing thoughts about blending. They will be anywhere from scared to angry, and anything between. We knew that we were following the Spirit. It was continually being reconfirmed that our decision to marry and begin to blend these two families was right. This was THE right time, and these were THE right families. It has taken patience, and sometimes it feels like a roller coaster ride. But little by little, the kids have trusted us and have shown strength and support in this worthy endeavor.

Justin

I too asked the heartfelt questions that had to be answered before Jen and I were married. "Do I love this person?" "Do we love to be together?" "Do we get along with each other?" "Do I want to be with this person for the rest of my life?" Yes, yes, yes, and yes?!!! From the night we met, I knew that if we put in the effort, our relationship would grow. As long as we stayed committed to making it work, we knew that despite the difficulties, we could come together and stay together.

Way back on our first date, Jen and I were out until about 1:30 a.m. We spent most of the time talking and telling the stories of our lives. We talked for so long that we missed curfew. Curfew? What should curfew be as an adult? Jen's kids were angry when she got home because she was out past midnight. When I talked to her on the phone the next morning, she said she didn't think things would ever work out. I was very confused until she told me about the uprising her kids had against her for staying out past the curfew that the children had set for her—midnight!

Desperate to find a way that I could see her again, I asked, "Would it be okay if I just came to your house and met your kids?"

"Yes, I think so," she answered.

"What did you tell them about last night?" I asked.

She replied, "I told them it was great."

"Did they ask if we kissed?"

"Yes" was her response.

"And what did you say?"

"Yes," she replied.

"Why did you tell them?! My kids were mad enough that we were even meeting. I can't imagine how they'd react if I said that I'd kissed you!"

She then said, "Well . . . they asked, so I said yes."

Finding time to be alone together, to talk about the intricacies and intimacies of our relationship has been a challenge from the beginning. We spent a lot of time when we were dating, reassuring our children we were still there for them. It was hard for all of them to accept a split between the time we spent with them and the time we spent alone together. There were anger and jealousy in some cases. Our kids still struggle with why we want to go on regular dates and work on our relationship.

Time is a gift that you should continually give one another in marriage. It's an ongoing way of saying, "You're important to me, and I love our friendship and romance." For us, the honeymoon period ended immediately after our short honeymoon was over. We came home to seven kids who needed us. Of course, even today we still need to have alone time together. We need time away from our kids to build upon our commitment to each other, our marriage, and our family. It's a must. Our alone time is cherished partially because there's so little of it.

Affection and Intimate Moments

Affection and intimacy could easily be discussed in the final chapter of this book, but because it's a bit of an issue from the beginning of a loving relationship, we will cover this delicate topic now. Jen and I did discuss intimacy back when we interviewed remarried couples about blending and received some hearty advice. But I'm only going to discuss our personal experience with it from the beginning of our relationship until the present day. And we can only scratch the surface of this subject that is incredibly important, and especially important to keep sacred.

The first sign of weirdness was when our children first saw us holding hands. On one of my trips to Utah early on, Jen and I held hands when we were at a mall with her children. Perhaps one of the reasons we chose to hold hands at that time was because we both hate going to the mall, so it was a perfect way to comfort each other in our shared anxiety. I was discreetly aware of the reactions in the eyes of her children. Their eyes told me that it looked awkward to them, which was very understandable. But they were also curious. Throughout the time that we dated, every time I pulled into Jen's driveway to take her home, I was aware that her kids were lined up along the living room window waiting to see if we would kiss. We always took care of the kissing part before I drove her home.

When Jen was visiting me and my children in California, the first holding-hands experience was equally puzzling to my children. We were in San Francisco walking through Pier 39, and naturally we began to hold hands. I could see my children looking back at us frequently, trying to understand how it was okay for their dad to hold hands with somebody other than their mother.

Both sets of children expressed their displeasure to the first signs of affection. The consensus was that we were acting like teenagers and moving way too fast. We weren't discouraged by our children's reactions because we had decided that no matter how long we waited to show affection, it would be the wrong time in the eyes of our kids. Yet we wanted them to see how a mature relationship could develop. Even if they felt that we were moving too fast. Eventually, we had to explain to them that holding hands, hugging, and kissing are essential parts of any loving relationship. Initially, it was hard for some of them to accept. Even today, some of them feel uncomfortable when Jen and I are affectionate. But that's okay. We are in fact married.

If our children hadn't seen us kiss previously, they certainly observed it when we made our vows. By the time we returned from our honeymoon, some of the children thought it was funny to joke about sex. In several cases, we found one or more of them listening at our bedroom door at night. In a couple of other cases, our door lock was picked. So one day when they were all gathered together, I told the kids that if they didn't want to hear or see anything that would be disturbing to them, they had better stay away from our door at night unless it was something urgent. Even in such cases, I told them that a knock at the door is a more effective way to get our attention than picking the lock and walking into our bedroom unannounced.

Relocation, Finding New Opportunities

Jen

As previously mentioned, Justin and his kids moved to Utah, leaving their home, schools, friends, and all that was familiar to them. I can't imagine how much apprehension it would cause for children who had clung to that security, especially after losing their mom. Justin's youngest daughter, Shay, was particularly sad to leave her home and friends to embark on a new journey. However, soon after Justin had told her that we were going to get married, she offered us full support and had faith. It's hard to be the "new girl." There have been times in which it has been difficult for her. But she continues to press forward with the conviction that we are a family. Since we would be staying in my home, it was a different challenge for his kids than it was for mine. Nonetheless, my children struggled also. My children were worried about what it would feel like to add four more family members to our home.

Justin

When Jen and I were discussing marriage, I was teaching at an inner-city high school in Sacramento. Teaching was a new career for me, and I knew that there would be opportunities to teach school in Utah even though the environment would be different. Along with career opportunities, I wanted to find ways for my children to continue on with activities that were important to them.

As the day of our marriage drew closer, I flew out to Utah so that Jen and I could meet with school counselors at the middle school and high school that my kids would soon be attending. We discussed academics, art, soccer, and other activities that they were currently involved with in California. By the time we got my two youngest kids enrolled in the next school year, I felt that we had done everything we needed to do to make the transition as easy as possible. But it wasn't easy by any means.

If I could have some moments back, I would have spent more time with Jen in finding ways to make her children feel comfortable with the moving process also. While it was true that they weren't being asked to leave their schools and their friends, they had to make space and adjust to having a family nearly double in size over-night. The map might have been laid out, but it was uncharted territory for all of us.

Opening the Door of Our Hearts and Our Home

Jen

It is important in blending two families to arrive at a place where bonding can occur. The children are used to the personality of their biological parent. It's not as though the new parent is replacing the previous father or mother. Ever. And that's an important distinction to explain to your kids. This new parent is another adult to love them, support them, and provide for them in the absence of their parent who has passed. It's been our experience that each of our children has bonded to their new stepparent at their own pace.

Justin

Before Jen and I were married I prayed that I would never let her kids down. What I meant by this was that I didn't want to go into a marriage unless I knew that I could be a positive influence in her children's lives. Ashamedly, some days I'm not, but they do know that I love them. Children want to feel love and secu-rity streaming continuously from both of their parental figures. Loving parents have the best interests of their children in mind. Obviously this takes work. "Becoming a stepfamily is a process, not an event." (Brown, "Growing as a Stepfamily," 61).

After Christ was crucified and resurrected, he visited the Nephites in America and taught them the same gospel that he'd taught his people during his mortal ministry. He also healed the sick and afflicted. Jesus knew that the multitude had great faith in him. He said, "Blessed are ye because of your faith. And now behold, my joy is full" (3 Nephi 17:20). Jesus has taught that our joy can be full just like his as he's explained, "that my joy might remain in you, and that your joy might be full" (John 15:11). It should be noted that these quoted scriptures teach us that our joy can be full. In the scriptures, Jesus never says "My heart is full" because one's heart can never be too full of love. A fullness of joy is a beautiful part of the plan of salvation. The difference in wording is striking in that our hearts can be filled with joy, while on the other hand our hearts can never be completely filled with love. It can always be added upon. Just like with Christ's heart, our hearts have no end of space for loving others, and our pool of loved ones can never become overpopulated. If we open our hearts, the love that we have for our new spouse and our stepchildren has no bounds. The more that we learn to love, the more our joy can be full.

One of the most important questions we should ask ourselves about becoming a new parental figure for stepchildren is this: "Is it possible for me to love my stepchildren in the way that I love my biological children?" In creating a new family unit, it's crucial that all of the children feel loved by both parents. From my own experience and the stories that I've heard and read of other blended families, there is a full spectrum of feelings you can have about your new stepchildren. This spectrum can range anywhere from "I love them as if they are my own," to "I'm trying to love them, but I actually resent them!" The latter statement is, in my view, a tragedy. Parental love is obviously what every child and stepchild needs to feel from an adult-to-child relationship. While dating, this kind of love may seem automatic, because you love the person that you are dating. In reality, our love for our stepchildren may come by degrees. If it does, it's best to pray that the degrees will come quickly.

As Jen has mentioned, your relationship with your new spouse is the most important matter, while *all* of the children are next on the list. This doesn't mean that the children don't come first or that you love your new spouse more than your children. Nothing could be further from the truth. But parents are the foundation of the family. Jen and I have had challenges in how our children have been raised in the past as opposed to how we want them to be raised in the present. Family discussions, as well as individual time, have to allow for children to be open about how they feel things are going. Whenever we meet in a family council and in personal interviews, we ask the same three questions: "What is going well? What is not going well? What can we do better?" The goal is to bring two family cultures together to create a new one. Creating a new family culture is a continual process of integration—of implementing ideas and learning what works.

Being remarried and already having kids with different habits, interests, and personalities is challenging. Children's behaviors are never fully under our control. Their opinions are even less so. The expression "Choose your battles wisely" comes to mind. Priorities become a matter of separating what is important from what's not important.

Jen and I didn't want to bring differences of opinion that would take away the ease of living on a day-to-day basis—but it happens. We have seven children between us, so things can get messy. With so many people under the same roof, harmony is a balancing act. Whether we like it or not, blending brings many factors to the forefront that were never second-guessed before. Herein lies the challenge of blending on a day-to-day basis.

It might not be difficult for you to love a child when they already love you, but if they don't love you and you're all living together, you may be in for a real treat. I'm referring to the kind of treat that is not sweet. Of course, you want to love and accept all of your combined children, but they might not immediately be willing to love and accept you or your help. You may feel that however far you extend yourself in reaching out to establish a connection, you could unknowingly be speaking a different language of love than they're accustomed to. In any case, it's important to reach out with the kind of loving compassion that the Lord can put into our hearts. But it takes patience to accept that it can still take time to connect. Ideally in months. Maybe in years. Possibly an entire lifetime.

Considerations

♡ How will you handle showing affection with your significant other in front of your kids? If there are things that make them feel uncomfortable, how will you address it?

♡ Are you committed to defining and redefining your commitment to your marriage with your children?

♡ How will you keep your children involved in the planning process of beginning a new life with another family?

PART 3

This New World

CHAPTER 11

How Do We Grow Together?

Coming together is a beginning; keeping together is progress; working together is success.

—Henry Ford

When you are remarried and you start living together, stark differences in daily life surface immediately. No one knows what it's like to help raise both their biological children and their new stepchildren until they're there, riding the carousel, feeling like the world is spinning. While it's true that in marriage a man and wife must work together to make sure that all the children feel loved and cared for, it's also true that some children may require more attention than others. Perhaps they are still dealing with the grief of losing a parent. Perhaps the changes are just uncomfortable for them. It should not be assumed that bringing in new family members (including a stepparent) will help them heal faster. Because chances are, it won't. At least not for everybody. Struggling children may begin to struggle even more. Children who aren't struggling might begin to struggle.

Children grow up fast, and you don't want to lose precious time with any of them. You want to bond with all of them. I believe that parents should communicate often about how each of the children is doing, and coordinate efforts in being there for each of them as much as possible. Bonding is not always about how much time you put into your relationships. Sometimes it simply comes down to the way in which you nourish your relationships daily. By nourishing your relationships, they become enriched and things begin to feel more natural.

Noel

Marriage and Mom

It doesn't matter how old you are when you lose a parent. It hurts, it's hard, and it feels like your world is crashing down. For me, losing a parent in high school was devastating. My mom didn't get to watch me graduate, she didn't get to watch me get married, she won't get to hold my kids . . . but I know that she is there. When I got married and sealed to my husband, I knew that my mom was there. These special moments are what hold you over. These moments are what help you to know that even though you don't have a parent here anymore—they are close.

I got married in the LDS temple in Payson, Utah. The Payson temple has these amazing, colorful, stained-glass windows. When I was sealed to my husband, I took a moment to look at these beautiful windows. I could see my mom shining through them, watching me. The glass lit up, and the colors came to life. I was grateful for this special moment. Some people have told me that I would have dreams about her. Unfortunately, all I've had are nightmares about her being sick. It feels like I'm reliving a horror movie. I wake up trembling until I realize it's not real anymore. She's gone. I haven't had any good dreams about her, but I have had some pretty special moments that help me know that she's close and watching over me.

My wedding day was an absolute dream. I was nervous because I thought I would have to plan everything myself. After all, I didn't have a mom to help me. I didn't think that Jen would want to help me because she has three daughters of her own to plan weddings for. Planning a wedding myself while in school and working and having no clue what I was doing was a terrifying thought.

After I got engaged, I cried at the thought that I wouldn't be planning my wedding with my mom like every little girl dreams about. Those tears came to an end really fast. Jen was willing to do literally anything for me. She would send texts each day asking me about colors, decorations, and food. She helped make all of my dreams happen. We used a friend's backyard for the reception, my aunts helped with the food, Jen worked with a lady to get decorations, she got the speakers from her bishop for music, and so much more.

I was beginning to freak out because Jen asked me what color of cutlery I wanted, and I didn't know if I wanted clear cutlery or gold. I never expected to be so worried about cutlery, but I'm so thankful that I got the chance to be! And Jen wasn't the only one who helped. Marie was willing to be the MC because I didn't want a DJ. Jen and Marie came wedding dress shopping with me. Marie helped organize little details and made sure the prices were okay. Jen and Marie helped my wedding to be the happiest day, when I thought it would be the most overwhelming day without my mom.

Don't get me wrong—it wasn't all perfect. I missed my mom tremendously. I felt empty without her. But seeing her through that stained-glass window and holding my heart necklace that we all got when she died—filled that empty space.

It's extremely weird to not know a family and then all of a sudden be living with them (as you might imagine). Of course, we all met before we lived together, but we didn't truly get to know each other. All we knew was that our parents were getting married and that my family was going to be living in their house. It was a confusing process. No one knew how to feel. Most of us were teenagers. We had our own lives, our own friends, our own schools, and we didn't want to change that.

"This wasn't supposed to happen!" is a thought that often crossed my mind. "I should have my mom with me, I should still be living in California, and I shouldn't have stepsiblings or a stepmom." What was going on?

How did this all happen? It was a very emotional day when my dad and Jen got married. Over the next few months, we tried to get to know each other better. We would often go out to eat or do something fun. It was pretty amazing that we were all so close in age. We found that we could relate to each other in a lot of ways, and we all had a very similar sense of humor. I think the biggest breakthrough came less than a year after my father and Jen were married.

For spring break we decided to plan a trip to San Diego. We rented a beach house, but when we got there the hot water didn't work. We called the owner and instead of coming to fix it, he told us he would move us into another beach house. It was a blessing in disguise because although the first beach house was great, the next one was absolutely amazing! It was right along the beach, brand new, and huge. There were windows that let a perfect amount of light in, and it was so clean.

We spent our week in San Diego at the beach house, at the beach, at the zoo, eating out, doing activities, and bonding. My favorite moment from our trip was when all of the siblings decided to walk on the boardwalk at the beach together. Jen and my dad stayed behind, and this was a moment the siblings truly bonded. We laughed, took pictures, saw a one-legged seagull, and saw a "water bender." As we walked along that boardwalk in a line of seven, I could just imagine our mom and their dad looking down upon us, smiling. It was a great trip and one that I will never forget.

It's possible to blend. It takes time, it's confusing, it's hard and sometimes sad, but it is possible. We have had our fair share of tears, laughs, and arguments. In the end, we know that this was the plan. Our parents were meant to meet, and we were meant to become siblings. Sometimes, we need our time alone. Some of us aren't even living at home anymore. But we are grateful to be a family.

Jen

Making Connections

Some of our children have embraced the stepparent relationship, and it's been a pretty seamless transition for them. One of my daughters has struggled at times. But not for Justin's lack of kindness toward her. He has attended many of her extracurricular activities and has shown support for her often. In having lost a parent to suicide, she, like my other children, has struggled with trust issues. This is understandable, and she is doing much better now. One awesome memory I have of Justin and my daughter was when she was working on a difficult essay for school. She approached him one evening for help. Justin has a talent for writing and she knew it.

The three of us were in our bedroom late that night as he critiqued her work and helped improve her essay until it was just right. I loved the fact that she reached out to him, and enjoyed watching her trust him in his abilities to help her. Days later, when she received her grade, she came home from school exclaiming, "Hey, Justin! WE got an A on my essay, and my teacher loved it!" She genuinely thanked him for his help.

Regardless of the work, love, and attention we've both given to each other's children, it takes time for bonding to occur. Trust must be established. We feel like we have progressed over the last three years of blending, but it takes work every day. Many beautiful moments have been spent together.

As Justin mentioned, we currently give the kids opportunities either in a family meeting or in a one-on-one talk to freely express how they feel things are going. They can share what they think is working and what they are struggling with. These discussions are vital to us as their parent and stepparent in order to more specifically focus our attention on each child's needs.

As parents, a mother and father have roles that differ in the family. We've both been given divine roles. Mothers are generally more nurturing, and fathers are generally more protective. Even with these differences, through time, bonding can occur for both parents. It may come sooner for some, but it will happen. It's been a beautiful thing to watch the evolution of it, but it hasn't been easy. Is it perfect now? No. But we have continued to commit to creating an atmosphere for this to happen. There have been challenging times. And there have been sweet moments of love and acceptance, and they continue to happen every day.

Justin

Communicating with Everyone

In The Book of Mormon, in the book of Mosiah, King Benjamin gathered all the people in Zarahemla so that he could address them before he passed away. His desire was to have the people see and hear him speak the truths of the gospel. The mass of people could not fit within the walls of the temple, so he had a tower erected on which he could preach to all the people of Zarahemla—men, women, and children. The people pitched their tents with the doorways facing the temple. Even so, not all could hear his words, so he had the preaching published throughout all the land (Mosiah 2:1–9).

The walls of the temple of Zarahemla can be compared to the walls of our homes. It's important that our communication about where we stand as a blended family is heard by every member whether the children are at home, attending college, on a mission, or even married with children of their own. In other words, we need to assure a way for all the children to see, hear, or read about how things are going. Acknowledge their concerns and struggles. Discuss what needs to be discussed. For those no longer living at home, you can always FaceTime, email, or text. It's good to have everyone in the loop so that everyone is on the same page with regard to family progress.

The Drive

Some of the most memorable moments with our blended family came early on in our marriage when we planned short trips together. There was some self-consciousness at first, as one might presume. We all wanted to be ourselves, and we tried to, with initial reservation. Jen and I created opportunities to watch our kids intermingle with each other. I realized that I knew very little about Jen's kids and she knew very little about mine. Jen and I continued to advocate for one another—to build each other up and share some of the qualities that drew us to each other. I told my kids what great qualities Jen possessed and that she cared for them. I'm certain that Jen was building me up in a similar fashion. We want them to know that we love each and every one of them.

It was also a time when our children needed constant reassurance. It was a new mindset that was difficult for each of them. Add to the mix that every child is different and each of them has their own personality. Again, add to the mix that each of the children is still trying to feel comfortable in their new lifetime relationships with each other. Also, add to the mix that each of them is in a different stage in the grieving process. Finally, add to the mix that the new stepparents are quite different from their deceased biological parents, so the relationships take time.

I learned a lesson very early on in our marriage that I will never forget. We were traveling in separate vehicles from our home to Saint George for a family vacation. Saint George is about a four-hour drive from South Jordan. My kids and I were following Jen and her kids on the highway. I had a new truck and was anxious to see how powerful the engine was. We were driving at a comfortable speed of about eighty miles an hour. About two hours into the drive we stopped at a service station. Jen told me that Ashlee was going to take a turn driving the Suburban. Ashlee had recently gotten a driver's permit. After entering the highway, it became clear that Ashlee was being very cautious, as she drove about seventy miles per hour. I became a little impatient and decided to pass them at a very high speed.

We arrived in Saint George about fifteen minutes before Jen and her kids did. I noticed when they got out of the Suburban that Ashlee was a little upset. I asked Jen what was wrong with her. She replied, "Well, she's a new driver, and she feels like her dad would have followed her to make sure she was doing okay." The thought had not crossed my mind, and I soon realized that if it had been one of my daughters driving with so little experience, I would have followed to make sure everything was okay. I was disheartened, as I could clearly see that I had made a mistake. Why hadn't I followed her? After all, she was my new stepdaughter, so why wouldn't I treat her the same as I would my daughters? Lesson learned. Care for all the children equitably.

A Plan Nearly Foiled

We had planned activities for every day that we were in Saint George. One of our plans was to go to Zion National Park. It's hard to plan activities that will please everyone in a family of nine. We wanted everyone to be with us on the day that we went to Zion National Park, but not everyone wanted to go. A couple of our kids wanted to stay at the condo and swim instead. This was a case of persistence meets resistance.

Jen and I thought it was a great plan and that it would be enjoyable to experience some extraordinary things like walking The Narrows, which is a small stream hemmed in by the split of a large mountain. I thought all three of my kids would want to go because they'd never been to Zion before, but not all of them wanted to. Jen's kids, on the other hand, had been to Zion several times before and we assumed that they would like to experience it again. But not all of them wanted to go either.

There was some complaining by a couple of the older kids. We reminded them that we wanted everyone to go with us, and we stuck to our plan. I'm sure that every parent knows that encouragement isn't always enough motivation for everyone to be on the same page. But Jen and I had decided that we would endure the embarrassment of having teenagers pout about having to do what we wanted them to do. We had set the bar that some things are not negotiable, like it or not. As it turned out, we did hear a lot of complaining, but it was well worth the effort just to be together as a family that day. Not every activity has to be all-inclusive for a family that is blending. Many times, with our busy lives it's just not possible. Everyone should, however, receive invitations to participate in family activities, and whenever possible everyone should be present for all family gatherings.

A Moment of Spontaneity

On one of the days in Saint George, I could feel some tension within the group. I pulled into a shopping center and parked in front of a Target supercenter. In an attempt to elevate the mood I exclaimed, "Okay, you all, we're here on a spending spree. We're gonna go into Target, and you can buy anything you want as long as the total is under twenty dollars. You have twenty minutes to find what you want, and I'll meet you at the cash registers. I'm gonna start timing once everybody is out of the car."

My words invoked some wonder, especially in Jen's kids.

Noel looked at everyone and said, "He's serious; he likes to do random things."

Everyone got out of the car, and a few of them started running to the front doors of the store. A couple of them grabbed baskets, while others walked straight in and looked for the best aisle to start in. I walked around the store to see who was picking up what. The boys went straight to the electronics. Colby realized that he wasn't going to find anything for under twenty dollars there, so he backpedaled to the candy. Grant was still there and showed me a video game that was about thirty dollars. He said it was a really good deal. "Nope," I said, "it has to be under twenty dollars." As I walked through the aisles, I noticed that three of our kids were congregated in the snack and candy aisles. Grant joined them.

As I scanned the rest of the store, I saw that two of the girls were looking at earrings, bracelets, and whatever trinkets are in the section that I never go in. I sent a text to everyone when there were five minutes remaining. The kids were doing remarkably well at budgeting their finds. The bonus was that it was an activity that everyone was happy to participate in. But when the time was up, nobody knew where little Kate was until we saw her round the corner at the opposite end of the store. Toys were spilling over the ends of her cart. She cried out for help, and Ashlee immediately went to help her. The rest of us watched as Ashlee started laughing. She came walking back to the checkout area as she smiled and said, "Kate thought that she could get everything she wanted as long as each item cost less than twenty dollars." We had a good laugh about it. But Kate wasn't laughing; she burst into tears.

Needless to say, I allotted her an extra ten minutes as she and Ashlee went back to restock the shelves in the toy section. With the help of Jen and Ashlee, Kate was led to the candy section, and she came out happy in the end. The lesson that I learned was that sometimes you must look outside the box and find some creative ways to have fun.

Becoming a Twinned Rainbow Family

After a rainstorm, a rainbow is often seen as the sunlight breaks through the clouds and reflects its light off the tiny droplets of water that remain in the atmosphere. The colors of the rainbow are always in the same order: red, orange, yellow, green, blue, indigo, and violet. Imagine if you walked outside one day and could see that the colors were changed and in the wrong order. The rainbow that has always appeared in a certain way is expected to continue to appear in the same way it always has. If the seven colors of the rainbow were to be scrambled, the order of reality would seem compromised.

Interestingly enough, nature sometimes produces a double (twinned) rainbow, which occurs when the sunlight is reflected off the water droplets twice and has a mirrored effect. A twinned rainbow consists of one rainbow with its seven colors appearing in the expected order, while the second rainbow is always seen with the seven colors inverted. They are opposites.

Like the colors of a rainbow, every family has a consistent order in the way they do things. Children thrive on both structure and consistency in the home. Like the order of the colors of a rainbow, the way things have worked in the family is what children become accustomed to as they get older.

We are a *twinned rainbow family* and proud of it. I was talking to Noel awhile back about how our family is unique, as we are composed of so many different personalities with so many struggles and so many accomplishments. Within the labels of the personality types, we represent all of them. We have children who are accomplished in academics, golf, dance, drill team, art, music, baseball, softball, soccer, writing, acting, singing, and production just to name a few. We try to keep the chaos beautiful, but we sometimes fall short. We've proven that we can handle many things, but sometimes many things handle us. Indeed, we are two rainbows, opposite of each other yet with everything in common.

Considerations

♡ How will you gauge where each of your children is at in blending?

♡ How will you help children who are struggling with their new circumstances?

♡ What is your plan to help everyone in the family feel connected?

♡ What is your strategy to resolve problems that arise?

CHAPTER 12

Lost and Found

Our sheep may be hurting, lost, or even willfully astray;
as their shepherd, we can be among the first to see their need.

—*Bonnie H. Cordon*

As a remarried couple, Jen and I continually seek to receive insight and inspiration from the Lord. We want our blended family to work for everyone. We believe that God can and does lead us toward a spirit of unification in the home. But it's only human to question hard things and why they are necessary for us to progress in this life. The purpose of God's plan is to taste the bitter and embrace the sweet. Ours is a world of adversity. As parents, we strive to raise our children in a manner that will ultimately be for their benefit whether they see it or not. In my opinion, one of the most heartbreaking things that a parent can witness is seeing children who willfully detach themselves from things of a spiritual nature and become unhappy as a result of making poor life choices. If our grieving children are feeling bitterness about the things they don't understand, it's still vital for them to know that they are still an important part of the family.

Accepting Our Children

When I was an only parent, there was a constant dialogue going on in my mind about what I could be doing to help my children make sense of the circumstances that they were faced with. In short, I never felt good enough to be raising three kids by myself. But I did the best I could under the circumstances. It's never too late for growth in knowledge and understanding, and it's never too late for a parent to simply accept their children as they are while continuing to help them find their way back from the dark places they've been.

It's important to consider that some children may comprehend the ways of the Lord sooner than others. Some may be constantly struggling to know their place in the Lord's plan. Some may completely go astray from the principles they've been taught their entire lives. It requires patience and foresight, as well as the kind of love that will never be revoked under any circumstances. "God never loses sight of our eternal potential, even when we do" (Stephens, "If Ye Love Me," 119). Indeed, a child who has suffered the loss of a parent may experience feelings that they are lost in life.

In the scriptures, we are taught that we can never stray so far as to eliminate the possibility of ever being found. Jesus said, "For the Son of man is come to save that which was lost" (Matthew 18:11). Such is the beauty of the Atonement; it is all-encompassing.

Children need to be assured and reassured that death is not permanent and that they will see their deceased parent again. It is up to us as parents to teach them these truths. The Lord has counseled us to, "establish a house, even a house of prayer, a house of fasting, a house of faith, a house of learning, a house of glory, a house of order, a house of God" (Doctrine and Covenants 88:119). Although we all fall short, this is the kind of house that we should strive to create. But even if we're doing what we feel is right as parents, it doesn't mean that our children will not go their own way for better or worse. Acceptance of this fact is vital if we are ever to take the necessary steps to be an all-inclusive family.

Difficult Times

By preparing for hard things, we become actively engaged in planning for happiness. Since Jen and I have been married, we've often explained to our kids that our marriage is an important part of our own eternal progression. If it wasn't, then we wouldn't have been prompted to get married in the first place.

Difficult things often happen before we realize the great things ahead of us. One might think, "I've had enough trials to last a lifetime. How could life possibly get any harder?" It takes strength to carry on, so much so that the thought of having any more trials is wearying at best. Anyone who has lost a spouse has experienced the kind of sadness that feels like dark clouds are looming overhead. One might think, "What else in life could go wrong?" The answer is anything. Anything can happen. This life wasn't meant to be easy. More struggles will come. You can count on it! Despite the sorrow of losing a loved one, we don't become immune to other trials and adversities. Trials don't stop to consider what we've already gone through and say, "They've had a tough life, let's skip this one and find somebody else to pick on." Elder Henry B. Eyring has said, "If you are on the right path, it will always be uphill" ("Raise the Bar," *Ensign*, January 25, 2005).

When my late wife Angie was diagnosed with cancer, just a day after she was released from the hospital, we were informed that her father had passed away. She began the grieving process of losing a parent as she began her fight with cancer. What a difficult set of circumstances. By sharing this story, I share the belief that we should prepare ourselves the best we can for any challenge regardless of where we are in life. When more trials come, how will we respond to them? It is the Lord's plan, and we are told that if we trust in him, we can overcome any and all hardships. But if we stray from our true convictions, we too can become like a sheep who is lost.

Parental Intervention

As a teacher, I had the responsibility of disciplining children who misbehaved in my classroom. In some cases, I would write up a disciplinary referral and send the student(s) to the office. When I wrote the referral, I would recommend what I thought the consequences of that student's actions should be, and I would let the principal or vice principal make the final decision. In some respects, what was called a disciplinary referral was more of an intervention for misbehavior.

If you are remarried with children, you've probably heard many times that you should only discipline your own biological children. Perhaps the word discipline feels limiting to you as a stepparent. However, sometimes a *disciplinary* action is not the same thing as a *consequence* set for a child. You might see certain behaviors that require immediate intervention, so you must take on the role of disciplinarian, regardless of whether you are the biological parent or the stepparent. For example, if two children are fighting, they both need to be disciplined immediately or they'll probably just keep on fighting. The discipline can come from you, while the consequences can later be decided on by the biological parent.

Sometimes, consequences can be set in advance and can make disciplining more proactive and simple. For example, Jen and I set a night that each of our children was expected to do the dishes. We were having trouble getting anybody to do the dishes on their assigned night, so we decided that anyone who missed their dish night wouldn't receive an allowance for that week. We told the kids what the rule was, and what the consequences would be.

Establishing rules and expectations is essential for any healthy, well-functioning family. We've found that with things like chores, if we let our children know the consequences in advance, it takes away the scenario of who should discipline whose children. If rules and expectations are set beforehand, many foreseeable problems can be resolved regardless of which parent is there to intervene.

The Pellet Gun Incident

On a particular occasion early on in our marriage, Grant and Colby decided that they would test the waters. Jen had bought a pellet gun because both boys have an interest in shooting. We didn't think there was any danger in taking the pellet gun out to the backyard to practice. But things got ugly fast as the boys began tossing up full cans of soda and blowing holes in them. After a couple of hours, Jen went out to the backyard and found that the stray pellets were putting cracks in the vinyl fencing all around our backyard. Jen took the gun away after we found approximately twenty holes in the fence. We were both upset with the boys. In this situation, the consequences were the same for both of them. We took the pellet gun away.

I decided to show some confidence in Colby and Grant as I gave back the pellet gun the next day, but this time I instructed them as to how to use it responsibly by giving them a proximity in which to shoot the gun. They were to shoot empty soda cans set on the ground. There would be no more shooting aimlessly at flying projectiles because there was no telling what the pellets would hit if they missed the target.

The boys spent about an hour doing target practice, and then they brought the pellet gun into the house. Ashlee was in the kitchen when the boys came inside. To this day, I don't know what the motives were when Colby decided to try shooting the pellet gun in the house. He blasted a hole in our leather couch in the family room. We immediately took away the gun again and said that they were no longer going to shoot anything. They were clearly testing the limitations. We knew that they had been shooting in the backyard again so we went out to see if they had done any more damage to the fence.

At first, we didn't see any new holes, but as we looked more closely, we saw small pieces of paper taped to the fence. This time, not only had they made more holes in the fence, they'd tried to cover them up. It was a laughable thing, but we weren't laughing. This incident began a new stage in learning how to discipline the kids together while the consequences were left for either parent to decide. Grant is Jen's biological son, so she handled the consequences with him. Colby is my biological son, so I handled the consequences with him. But one thing was certain, neither one of them was ever going to see that pellet gun again.

Our way of separating discipline or intervention from consequences has worked out well for us at times. While Jen and I don't hand out disciplinary referrals the way a school teacher would, we do discuss the problems and misbehaviors that have taken place. Sometimes we also give suggestions to each other about what we think the consequences should be if two parties are involved. Also, if Jen comes to me about a problem with one of my kids that needs to be addressed, I want to know her story about the incident. In fact, I want to hear it from her before I talk to my child about the situation.

But ultimately, I assign the consequences for my own biological children, and she decides the consequences for her children.

New Family, New House, New Everything

When Jen and I announced to friends and family that I would be moving to Utah, despite hearing opinions that we should buy a new house to live in together, I moved into the house that Jen owned. It was practical. Eventually, however, the home that Jen and her children had lived in for twelve years became a place where sad memories were surfacing. Sometimes it's hard to make new memories when you're stuck in an old place.

We decided it was time to find a place that we could call ours. We prayed that we would find a house that we would love and would have a bedroom for everyone. Those were our concerns. The first day we spent looking at homes we found one that we all agreed would be our place of refuge from the world.

Anytime you have two families moving all their belongings into one space, rest assured that it will be a nightmare. Things will be misplaced. Things will be broken. Things will disappear forever. I was afraid that once we got all of our old furniture, linens, decorative pieces etc., into a new house, everyone would decide they wanted new everything else to match the house. Jen assured me that wouldn't be the case—but it was the case.

Not long after we moved, we started selling our old furniture and buying new furniture to replace it. Gradually, other old things were vanishing as new things appeared: new decor, new pictures, new couches, new chairs, and so on and so forth. Within a few months, all of the moving and assembling of new furniture had been done with the exception of Shay's room. So one day I said, "Okay, Shay, let's go spend some money at IKEA." At IKEA she found a bed frame but it would need assembling. When we got home I began to put together some hardware and pulled out the instruction manual—but it wasn't in English. In fact, it wasn't in any language at all; it was simply a pamphlet of bad illustrations.

I could see Shay watching my progress from the corner of her eyes. She said she didn't expect me to finish the work in one night. But I envisioned seeing her happily lying on her new bed, content and appreciative of the time I spent in putting it together. The instructions for the assembly recommended the use of a screwdriver so as to not crack the wood on the headboard. I decided to use a power drill instead for faster assembly, I set a screw on the drill bit, put it in place, and I cracked it!

I immediately started to cry and said, "We might have to go back to IKEA and buy another bed frame."

She asked, "Why are you crying, Dad?"

I didn't know how to answer. Jen came into the room when she heard me sobbing.

"Justin, what's wrong?" she asked.

Through my tears, I showed Jen the part of the board that had split.

She said, "You're such a nice dad. We can fix it with some wood glue."

Jen and Shay reassured me that the mistake I'd made was okay. The only person that was hurting was me. From the time that I became a widower, I wanted to remove all obstacles, problems, and difficulties that were in the path of my children. I wanted to buy them things so that I could see a smile on their faces. I wanted to fix everything in their world, but I couldn't. I wanted things to go perfectly for them, but, in reality, things never do.

Since the night of my meltdown while putting Shay's bed frame together, I've realized that my desire to do everything right as a father is a standard that I can't live up to, but it's okay. It's okay to let small things go. It's okay to break things because they can be fixed. A cracked bed frame is not worth crying over.

Considerations

♡ What will you do if a child refuses to obey the rules of the household?

♡ How will you handle things if children just don't get along?

♡ How will you make sure that every child in the family feels accepted?

CHAPTER 13

I Do - We Do - You Do: A Model for Teaching

The best way of teaching is learning together.

—*Pranav Acharya*

In the field of education, there is a comprehensive strategy that allows for a gradual release of responsibility from the teacher to their students. The idea behind the I Do-We Do-You Do is that the teacher gives direct instruction to the class, which is the "I Do" phase. The learning goals and responsibilities are set forth, and then the teacher models what is being taught. The students are to listen and take notes on what they are learning.

In the "We Do" activities, the instruction is based on guided interaction with students. The teacher provides prompts and clues by asking questions to check for understanding. In the "You Do" phase, each student works independently, which helps the teacher determine the level of understanding that the students have achieved. It is the students' responsibility to show what they have learned from the lesson. Of course, every student is at his/her own level of comprehension, and it's up to the teacher to provide feedback or to reteach portions of the lesson that students have not yet mastered.

Marriage and family life can be approached in a similar fashion. The act of getting remarried is like saying "I Do" accept all the responsibilities that go along with leading our new family by example. In families that are blending, direct instruction goes with the territory. They need to be taught gospel principles and what their responsibilities are as members of the family. Goals should be set out in a way that children will understand them. The "We Do" model is a participatory role in carrying out the goals that are set. For example, "We Do" have family prayer together. "We Do" show respect for each other. "We Do" have jobs that need to be done. The "You Do" phase allows us as parents to continually assess the situation and to reteach or make modifications as they are needed. Are things going as planned? If not, what can be improved upon?

As Jen and I once prepared for a family meeting, we decided to take the kids through the house to show them where the cleaning products were. Then, we demonstrated the steps that were to be taken when cleaning the bathrooms. We showed them where to put the dishes when they were unloading the dishwasher and what to do with the dishes when they're dirty. We even showed them little things like taking the lint out of the dryer before drying the next load of laundry. One might assume that such simple things could be done correctly just by telling the children to do them. But these assumptions can be obliterated when the kids all say their chores are done and the house looks roughly the same as it did before they started doing them.

Deal or No Deal

Time, care, and concern take center stage with regards to parenting children and nurturing a new marital relationship. There is no quick fix for some of the differences that inevitably arise due to the recent changes that make up a "new normal" atmosphere in the home. A new normal can take root only if there is love in the home. Challenges can come quickly, and they often do. If there are rifts between family members, everyone can feel it, and it becomes stressful for everybody. As with anything, these hard moments are there to be learned from.

As Jen and I have read posts in private chat rooms written by remarried widows and/or widowers, we've caught wind of a term that one party or another has used in the midst of blending families. The term "deal breaker" is a somewhat common response to a conflict between couples who are dissatisfied with their new situation. Marriage is a partnership of love and respect. It's not like a business deal where you shake hands on a golf course after you make a sale—it's ongoing.

Saying something is a deal breaker is a simple way to draw a line by saying, if things continue as they are, then all bets are off and the vows made in marriage are going to be purposefully broken. For example, if one parent doesn't agree with the behaviors or discipline of the other parent's children, it could be labeled as a "deal breaker." Remarriage is difficult, and the most common reason that a partner becomes dissatisfied with a family situation is children. Children have the power, whether they know it or not, to make a parent second-guess their decision to remarry.

When a spouse expresses that something is a deal breaker, it's essentially saying they're willing to divorce over it. In essence, one is saying, "If you don't change this for me, then it's over between us. So fix it or else!" When you bring children into a marriage, it's always a challenge. There are no exceptions, and there's no way around it. If a couple is constantly at odds with each other because of their children, it can cause a strain in the marital relationship and can potentially cause that marriage to fail.

Making It Work

On a particularly difficult weekend early on, I was frustrated with the kids because I was tired and wanted a Sunday nap, and they kept knocking on the bedroom door. I vented my frustrations about everything and walked down to the basement where it was dark and quiet. Instead of falling asleep on the couch, I began texting Jen about how it was unfair because all our kids had the privacy of their own rooms and I didn't. By the time I walked back upstairs, one of Jen's daughters was crying to her because she felt like I didn't love her.

When I looked at Jen she said, "I don't think this is gonna work."

I composed myself and replied, "If it feels like it isn't gonna work, it means that we're not working hard enough."

Admittedly, the person who wasn't working hard enough was me. Now when Jen and I are faced with challenges in our marriage, we evaluate how hard we're working at it. Are we using time on Sundays to have gospel discussions? Are we reading the scriptures together as a couple? Are we attending the temple? Often we find that there are many things we aren't putting sufficient effort into. Taking spiritual inventory and immediately acting on it has literally saved our family.

The Love for the Lawn

In California, I used to have the most beautiful lawn in the neighborhood. I did a thorough job of keeping the lawn nicely cut and edged every Saturday. I'd planted tulips of many colors and honeysuckle plants in the front yard. I trimmed the bushes and plants with care. My backyard had palm trees and lush greenery. I also had a small garden of vegetables and strawberries. I took pride and joy in caring for our yard.

As Angie was battling cancer, my front yard became an eyesore to the neighborhood. Parts of the lawn had died where sprinkler heads were broken. Plants were dying because the drip lines were no longer adjusted to provide them with enough water in the summer. One day as Angie and I came home from a visit with the oncologist, I noticed that church members had planted new flowers and shrubbery in the open spots of the yard where plants had withered and died. It lifted our spirits. However, as time went on, the new plants also began to wither and die.

In the spring, I noticed that there were many blossoms on the leaves of my mandarin tree so I began to water it again. Soon enough, a lone blossom had budded and grown on the tree. When the day came that I picked the small piece of fruit, I was so excited that I told my family that we were going to have a treat after dinner. The whole family was excited to see what the treat was that I had planned for us. I peeled and plated the small piece of fruit. I exclaimed, "Here's our dessert!" The kids were laughing at my excitement. We each took a wedge of the mandarin. I savored the taste. It was sweet, as I had let the mandarin orange grow until it was ripe. It amazed me how much work I had done for one little piece of fruit. I began to feel hope that I would be able to revive the rest of the front and backyards.

But within six months of Angie's passing, our front and backyards became overgrown with weeds. The plants were untrimmed, and my grass had also become patchy with weeds. Then one day my kids and I weeded the front yard. Noel and Shay stood on the sidewalk and displayed a weed that had grown taller than either of them. We laughed and took a few pictures of them holding the weed up as it stood upright about a foot above their heads. Unfortunately, one day of care wasn't enough to save the yard.

The first time Jen came to visit, I was apologetic about the way that my front yard looked. It was embarrassing. Not only was the front yard in shambles, but the inside of our house was in complete disarray. Jen suspended judgment, for which I was grateful.

In contrast, the first time I saw Jen's lawn it looked immaculate. The grass was a lovely deep green, and the bushes were trimmed. The sprinklers covered the entire area of grass. I was impressed to hear that Grant had kept up the lawn the way his father had before he passed away. In July of that year, after Jen and I were married and we'd all settled into her home, the lawn began dying in spots, and I couldn't figure out why. It was getting plenty of water.

I recall Grant saying to Jen, "Dad would be so mad if he saw the grass." I felt responsible for not keeping the grass up to par the way his father had. My embarrassment became deeper as we came home from church one day and Ashlee commented, "We're becoming the house with the ugly front yard." I began searching for answers as to why the grass was dying. In the subdivision that we lived in, there was great pride of ownership. Everyone else's grass was green and flourishing. I began to inquire of neighbors as to what they were doing to keep their grass alive.

Then one day, a neighbor explained to me that there was a system of fertilization he used to keep his grass beautiful. It was a simple thing, and with great anticipation I went with Jen to the local nursery and bought the fertilizer that the grass needed. Although it would never look as good as it did when Stoney was alive, I did my best not to let everyone down by becoming the house with the ugly front yard.

With such a simple effort the lawn was green again. I believe that our lawn restored some confidence that my stepchildren had in my ability to keep some things the way they had always been. Although the lawn lacked the boldness that my stepchildren were accustomed to, the effort that I put into restoring the health of the front and back lawn was well worth it. My lawn effort applies to blending in a general way. Even though things may not be done the exact way that a parent did them in the past, each consideration made by a stepparent to care for something that the children are attuned to can be a great way to restore some of their security.

Doing Holidays and Other Memorable Days, Together

One of the blessings of having a blended family is that siblings have the opportunity to learn empathy at a young age and carry it for life. It's like an acute awareness that enables them to comfort each other in times of need. For our seven children, the most tender and difficult days are Father's Day and Mother's Day. It's a struggle for everyone, but there is a degree of understanding present between siblings on those days. They have developed intuition to nurture each other when the burden is heavy.

Each of our children experiences difficult days in which there's no indication as to why they're having a tough time. Nevertheless, our children seem to understand that the sadness which may appear to others as just a bad day, is usually tied to memories of a time when their deceased parent was there for them. As parents and stepparents, we too struggle with sad memories, especially when we feel like we aren't doing enough to keep our children feeling happy. The struggle is continual.

Before Jen and I were married, for Mother's Day my kids and I received a large package from Jen and her kids. It was meant to lighten our hearts, and it did. The package that we received was filled with all kinds of great things. There were candies, popcorn, DVDs, and other thoughtful gifts. On a day in which nobody else had acknowledged my children and the hurt they felt in losing their mother, it was nice to receive something that told us that there were people out there who understood what losing a parent feels like. Of course, when Father's Day came, Jen and her kids received a package from us. It was a mutual acknowledgment that we too could empathize with the feelings of losing a parent.

There is a time of the year that is meant to be special and memorable beyond ordinary days of the year—a season of giving and spending time together as families develop traditions for all to enjoy. It is Thanksgiving and the holiday season in which we celebrate Christmas. Christmas is a particularly meaningful holiday, as Christians all over the world unite to celebrate the birth of our Savior. As a culture, we enjoy the beautiful Christmas lights that adorn the trees along the streets in town, the classic Christmas carols that are heard throughout department stores, the sweet smell of cinnamon, peppermint, and pine that seem to linger at every public square. Many families enjoy making gingerbread houses, decorating Christmas trees, and making goodies for the neighbors. And of course, Santa Claus makes appearances in malls, parades, and other festive places. Indeed, it's a time of unity in the family. Everyone has favorite Christmas shows to watch at home. Many people love to go out to see the Nativity scenes and Christmas light displays.

At this wonderful time of year, when I was a lone widower, my children still felt the sting of grief, and so did I. I knew that the holidays could cause them to delve deep into mourning. But Christmas isn't meant to be a time of sadness. I didn't strive to change anything. We decorated the Christmas tree together. Outside we had strewn the house and trees with lights. I put some of the presents under the tree early, just the way we had always done it.

I'd decided early on in the first year to let it be a time to accept the service that others were graciously giving. We attended family dinners, and I never asked what I should bring to the meals. Attending functions was enough. I didn't have the strength to be anything other than me in the present moment. Fortunately, the Relief Society president from our church in Lincoln was willing to do the bulk of the Christmas shopping for my children, and she even wrapped the presents. They looked amazing.

By the third Christmas after Angie's passing, we were in a blended family, and it did much to help with the occasion. There was more laughter and less silence. But being in a blended household can be another difficult change. The Christmas season truly is a time that tugs hard on the heartstrings. It's been said that during the holidays the blended family ought to develop new traditions together. Whether or not new traditions are put into place, there will be new traditions nonetheless.

When children are young, traditions are directed toward activities that they'll enjoy. The imprinted joy that children feel about past Christmas magic may fade because children get older and want to make new memories. Every year is a new phase of life in every family. Some of the old traditions may no longer interest them. While some traditions will always be desired, other traditions are bound to replace some of the old ones. When is it time to do away with the Elf on the Shelf? Probably when nobody thinks it's fun to look for him anymore.

During our first holiday season together, Christmas was a new kind of difficult, as the children tried to sort through and separate what great things are worth remembering and what great things can yet be built upon. However, new traditions are not meant to overshadow the norms of old traditions. In fact, many of the traditions that our blended family participates in are additions to traditions.

For example, during our first Christmas season together, both of our families upheld the tradition of making gingerbread houses. So instead of making one gingerbread house, we made two. Also, all seven of our children had always enjoyed opening one present on Christmas Eve. So we did it. In some ways, there isn't a need to start new traditions when the old ones are already in place. The similarities that our traditional families had once enjoyed carried over to our new family. However, it's important to make a distinction between what traditions can be enjoyed and what traditions can cause pain if they are continued. Some of the old traditions of a family can become a trigger for new trauma as children sometimes hold memories to be a sacred thing that they want to remember experiencing only with their deceased parent.

We must always consider that Christmas is meant to be a celebration of the birth of our Savior, Jesus Christ. That is a constant that will never change, and it's an anchor to which all Christmas traditions should be attached. The reading of the biblical story of the birth of Jesus is always appropriate. The Nativity scenes are meant to remind us of what Christmas is really about. We did our best to keep the Christmas season a time to focus on the birth of Christ. To remember that it is Christ—not Santa—that makes Christmas magical.

Like it or not, Christmas in a blended family is different. On the morning of our first Christmas together, as the kids looked at the presents around the tree, Ashlee and Kate noticed that something was different. All the presents under the tree were wrapped. The tradition in the Winterton family had always been that the presents from Santa were never wrapped.

"Santa didn't come," I heard Kate say.

I turned to Jen with a look of surprise as she said, "The ones from Santa were never wrapped."

Of course, they all knew that Santa Claus isn't real. But the excitement of seeing the unwrapped presents wasn't there. I'm sure there was some emptiness associated with it. Personally, I'd never heard of Santa leaving the presents without wrapping paper on them. A subtle difference, yes . . . but a difference nonetheless.

Our Missionary

One of the greatest blessings on our first Christmas together came from Marie, who was serving a mission in Arizona. The missionaries in her mission were given an hour to Skype with family on Christmas Day. When the time came, we all gathered around the computer to see and talk to her. We told her about how the family was doing and asked her questions about her mission. Jen, Ashlee, and Kate were so excited to see her that they crowded around the monitor so closely it was as if they wanted to reach through the screen and touch her.

As I sat back and listened, I learned of ways in which she'd been using her talents to inspire investigators and members of the Church in her area. Her sense of humor opened many doors and made people feel comfortable. She was a devoted missionary. During our Skyping session, she made us all smile and laugh, which provided us with comfort that she was doing what's right. On that day, I felt that we were all doing what was right, and it gave me a feeling of peace. She wasn't just a missionary, she was our missionary.

Together with the In-Laws

Jen and I have been fortunate in that the in-laws from our previous marriages have accepted our remarriage from the very beginning. We felt that keeping our kids in contact with our in-laws would assure our children that their deceased parents not only still exist, but that they can be formally acknowledged as an integral part of our lives.

On our first Thanksgiving together, we were invited to celebrate with Angie's family. We drove to Idaho to stay at my brother-in-law's house for the celebration. This was an occasion that we expected all our kids to attend. We wanted everyone to know that we were doing well as a family and that we were united on these special occasions. One of Jen's children was opposed to going at first because she felt it wasn't a part of her family in any way. But from the time that we arrived at my in-laws' house until Thanksgiving Day, she said that she felt that she was accepted and loved by Angie's family. We were all there together, and we were all made to feel welcomed even though a key figure of our family was not there physically.

On our first Christmas together, we had the opportunity to spend part of Christmas Eve with Jen's in-laws. We again expected all of our family to attend. This time there was some resistance from my kids about spending time with a family of strangers. I asked my children how they would feel if Jen's kids rejected Angie's family.

Jen and I could understand why our children would think it was awkward to be around Angie's family, or Stoney's family, but we felt it was important to spend some time with them. Being with Stoney's family was another successful visit. Within minutes of our arrival on Christmas Eve, my children felt accepted and that the in-laws were now a part of our support base.

Considerations

♡ As parents, how will you model correct behavior to your children?

♡ How are you expanding old traditions and creating new ones?

♡ What will you do if you have children who refuse to participate in family activities?

CHAPTER 14

Prepare for Hard, Plan for Happiness

i woke up thinking the work was done
i would not have to practice today
how naive to think healing was that easy
when there is no end point
no finish line to cross
healing is everyday work

—Rupi Kaur

The Morning of a New Beginning

The night prior to our wedding we had a solemn moment that none of us will ever forget. Everyone gathered in the living room of Jen's house. Our soon-to-be family of nine knelt in a circle and we had our first true family prayer. In that moment, the fears, uneasiness, and the unknowns left everyone for a time.

We were united in purpose, and I knew the anxieties of the children were temporarily lifted as feelings of unity entered our hearts.

This was what Jen and I had been working toward for eight months. A feeling of purpose and hope filled our hearts with the gentle calm that the Holy Ghost brings when humility is shown before God. There were no tears—there was only the peace of a confirmation that everything was right. I took the lead and prayed that God would shower his blessings upon us. So many prayers that had been offered by friends throughout our communities on behalf of our two families were being realized in that moment; prayers that our families would be comforted in the midst of our trials and anguish. We were becoming one family in a way that was a bit unconventional but seemed traditional in most respects.

After our prayer, the anticipation of what was ahead for all of us was pacified by peace in our hearts. It was an emotional moment in the most positive way of knowing that all would be well. We couldn't fathom the trials and difficult times that we would have in the future, nor did we attempt to at that time. It was a moment in which we were living in the present. We were where we needed to be.

On the morning of our wedding day, Jen sent me and the boys to drop off a trailer full of tree stumps that would be fashioned into seats. They were to be used around a fire pit to roast marshmallows for s'mores. As my boys and I pulled into the driveway leading to the backyard venue, I saw the chairs where people would be seated for the wedding. At the back of the seating was a beautiful trellis of wood laced with decorative flowers. It was rustic and lovely.

"No way!" I said to the boys, "Look at this place."

The original plan for our civil ceremony was to have a small wedding of about fifty spectators. But as I looked around, I saw well over a hundred chairs set up for guests, and there were about ten large round tables being set up for the reception.

What I saw was much, much larger than I had anticipated and more beautiful than any wedding and reception venue that I'd ever seen. The scenery made me feel insufficient for the occasion. It made me nervous to think that we would be having a wedding in front of nearly two hundred guests—most of which I had never met.

I immediately called Jen and said, "This was supposed to be a small wedding—this is huge! There are more than a hundred chairs lined up. This is not a small wedding, and I'm not the president preparing to give a State of the Union address."

There was a long silence at the other end of the phone as I said, "I can't walk through an aisle with this many people that I don't know watching me. I'll trip and fall on my face."

This was not the reaction that Jen had expected from me. I quickly realized that I'd hurt her feelings. She had put so much work into making it a perfect wedding.

But I continued, "I thought we were only inviting fifty people."

She sounded hurt as she said, "I know, but people kept asking when the wedding was because they wanted to come."

I said, "Yeah, but you don't understand; I only invited family and a few friends from California. I don't know your friends. I'm nervous already, and I don't like the idea of being in the spotlight in front of so many people."

She responded, "Honey, a lot of people pitched in, and a lot of people have asked if they could come. I couldn't say no to everyone. You don't need to be nervous. They're friends of my family and have been for years."

"I'm sorry," I responded apologetically. "It's just that this is not what I'd expected."

She asked, "What do you want me to do?"

I said, "It will be good. You've done well. We're going to take the logs out of the trailer and set them up and see what else needs to be done."

As we started hauling things out of the trailer, I could see people placing the round tables, putting tablecloths on them, placing centerpieces, hanging up lights over the tables, and putting together trays of food and desserts. It truly was amazing. At the entrance to the walkway leading to the trellis, there were barrels on each side. On one of the barrels, there were two large wooden letters painted white. There was a *W* for Winterton and an *E* for Eller. Together the letters spelled *WE*. Directly across there were two white letters that spelled *DO*. The decorations alongside the rows of seats consisted of ribbons and flowers all the way down the aisles.

Toward the back of the venue, there was a man setting up stereo equipment for dancing, and behind him I could see a gazebo with the wedding cake and a sign that said, "Mr. & Mrs." I asked several of Jen's friends what else the boys and I could do to help.

"Let's see," one of them said. "You could help finish putting up the chairs."

"More chairs?" I asked.

"Yes," she said.

There were more chairs to set up on both sides of the trail for the procession. I began to get nervous again, as there were nearly two hundred seats set up by the time we finished.

As I gazed at the scene before me, I began to think about the things that I had said to Jen, and I felt bad. I knew I'd hurt her feelings. This was, after all, one of the most special occasions of our lives. She'd done a splendid job preparing the wedding to be just as she'd pictured it. As the boys and I got back into my truck, I decided I should call Jen and apologize again for the things I'd said. I told her that she'd done an amazing job and that everything was beautiful. She knew that my apology was heartfelt and accepted it.

A New Story Begins

Jen

Justin and I decided on a civil marriage. The beauty of it cannot be described in words, but the benefit of it can. We were engaged on the first of June and married July 15, 2017. But prior to our engagement, I'd already had the wedding plans underway. Some of my closest friends helped me plan each detail. When I arrived before the ceremony, everything I saw was breathtaking. They had been setting up and decorating all day in the hot July sun. I was so grateful for their kindness and love.

We were married in a civil ceremony in a friend's backyard. There were several reasons why we wanted to be married civilly. We wanted our children to be present and to participate in the wedding. Years earlier, my wedding to Stoney took place in the Salt Lake Temple. My dad was not able to be there. Only my mom was there. After Stoney's death, my dad, along with my brothers, had been my rock of support throughout that trying time. They were very supportive and happy about Justin and I getting married and blending families. We also felt very grateful that many of our in-laws from both families attended the wedding and showed their support.

In the civil ceremony, my dad walked me down the aisle. In 2016, we had lost my mom, Stoney, and my oldest brother, Jeff. With my dad and my brothers, along with other family members, we had planned three funerals that year. The event of my wedding to Justin was the first happy time in which we could celebrate a tangible, amazing experience. Many tears were shed, but the most present emotion that I felt was joy. Our wedding day felt as if my heart had come full circle. I was in love and ready to marry Justin and begin our journey with him and his kids.

Each of our children was experiencing mixed emotions that day. They were supportive and happy and yet somewhat reluctant. Each of them had moments where they were thinking of their parent who had passed. I believe that each one of them at times was unsure how to feel. But many moments that day were memorable, and we bonded as we took family photos, danced, took pictures in a photo booth, roasted s'mores, and enjoyed the party. We all have very fond memories of that day.

Justin knew only a few of our nearly two hundred guests. He had a handful of friends and his family there. The rest of the guests in attendance were friends and family of mine, each of which had been a part of our sorrow when Stoney had passed. It thrilled them to be a part of such a loving ceremony and celebration. Hope was restored to our two families that we could be happy again, and that the Lord knows us and has shown that he knows how to best care for our families by bringing us together to create one family.

Justin

When I revisit the first pictures that were taken before the wedding ceremony, I see what things were happening that were outside of my view that day. Jen and the girls were working together, helping my soon-to-be bride put on her wedding dress, touching up her hair, and putting on jewelry. I didn't know at the time that Jen was wearing pearl earrings and a necklace in memory of her mother who had passed away before we'd ever met. Jen later explained that her mother's jewelry was a reminder that she was there in spirit with an ability as it were to peer through her side of the veil and see the important moments of Jen's life.

Then there are the pictures of me, alone in a room wearing suit pants, lacing up my shoes, tying, untying, and retying my tie so that it would be at the perfect length, landing at the center of my belt buckle. When the photographer left the room, I was alternating between trying to fix my tie and sitting in a chair sorting through note cards, trying to memorize the things that I would say to the guests after the ceremony.

At some point, I laid my note cards on a dresser in the order that I wanted to memorize them, reading and rereading my notes. I looked up and stared at my image in the mirror, and I started on my tie again. My father and brother-in-law Jasen walked into the room and asked if I was okay.

"I'm nervous, Dad," I answered.

He helped me get my tie to where I wanted it and, pointing to the note cards said, "Don't worry about what to say. It will come to you."

They offered a blessing of support, and I really appreciated it. As they blessed me, I once again received the peaceful confirmation that what was taking place was approved of the Lord and supported by the loved ones who had gone before me, and the loved ones who were before me, waiting for the procession to begin.

All seven of our children were participating in the wedding. and that was fantastic. The girls were Jen's bridesmaids, and the boys were the groomsmen. I had yet to see my bride in her wedding dress. The boys and

I first made our way outside to the split between the aisles of guests who were there waiting for the wedding to begin. I could hear the harpist begin playing a song called "One." The lyrics of the song started running through my head.

As Colby and Grant began to walk toward their places to the right of the lattice, I saw my brother standing in the center, as he was the clergyman who would conduct the ceremony. While walking between the aisles, my feet were light, and I felt a sense of dignity that I had not felt in a long time. Soon after, I was positioned on the right side under the trellis. I watched our five daughters continue the procession, all wearing beautiful matching dresses of pastel pink. Four were carrying bouquets of flowers, lining up on the opposite side of the boys.

I then watched as Kate was walking, tossing white rose petals. Lastly, I saw Jen smiling, being escorted by her father to the other side of the trellis. Before our eyes met, I scanned the rows of guests and saw my parents and siblings, Jen's siblings, members of my in-laws' family, members of Jen's in-laws' family, and many other guests that had come to witness the ceremony. It was an awesome sight. I then turned to Jen and looked into her distinctive blue eyes. She had a look of trust and happiness.

There are pictures of Jen and I standing face-to-face, holding each other's hands as my brother was leading the ceremony. I remember trying to memorize every word that he was saying so that I could remember what vows we were making. They were so simple and direct—so easy to make. The photographer took a picture of each of our children watching the ceremony. When I look at their pictures, I see mixed emotions in each of them. There were smiles and there were tears. It's apparent now that some of our children were taking it on faith, and others were taking it on trust. After we made our vows, we exchanged rings, we kissed, and we enveloped each other in love and respect.

I didn't end up using my note cards as I addressed the guests and expressed my gratitude to them for being there. I also expressed my love and thankfulness for Jen. It was much simpler to speak the words from the heart rather than by memory. I can't recall what Jen said as she spoke, but I do know that she's always said the right words at the right times. The most heartwarming picture of that day was our first family hug. Seeing us huddled together leads me to believe that a family hug lasts a lifetime.

We then gathered into a common area where Marie proposed a toast. I can't recall what she said, but I am still moved by the image of her addressing our guests and acknowledging the happiness that we all felt in that tender moment.

When Jen and I look at the pictures of our kids together at the wedding, we see strong individuals of all shapes and sizes. Our five girls standing and smiling in between our two boys, who were standing as if they were bookends, holding the group together. There are memories of the photographer herding all nine of us together, trying to fit every one of us into the frame. I remember her saying, "Okay, everybody move in a little closer." The closer we got, the more safety we felt as a whole.

The culmination of celebrating the moment was the dance of the bride and groom. Jen and I had never danced with each other before. As we danced, I looked back at the gazebo where we had cut the cake. I again saw the wooden sign that had been placed on the table which read, "Mr. & Mrs." All that had taken place that day was the accomplishment that two former strangers had fought long and hard to create; a celebration of our new life together.

When our song was over, we invited all who wanted to dance to join us. Parents, siblings, and friends broke down any apprehension that remained. The awkwardness that had existed at times throughout the months of dating and encouraging our children to bond, began to dissipate until it disappeared. Our children unleashed the energy of the moment. The pictures that captured this space in time still remind us of the new story that began to be written that day.

Our Time

So here we are! Life has taken on a new course. We've been blending for over three years now, and it is still just the beginning of our new voyage together. Despite choppy waters and cresting waves, our ship appears to be sailing in the right direction (most of the time). There have been moments when I've stopped and thought to myself, "Is this truly Heavenly Father's eternal plan of happiness?" However, despite the hard times, I choose to relinquish my fears when they enter my mind because every time I step back and observe our lives, I see that we all know it's been right all along. The events in our lives together continuously weave between hardness and happiness.

We are nine individuals that make up one family. Every member of our family has strengths that are easily recognizable. It's recognizing the blessings that sometimes takes further examination on our part. It's an everyday thing. Our children are beginning to embrace the sweetness and leave the bitterness behind. In the midst and tumult of uncertainty, sadness, pressure, anxiety, despair, and all other difficulties, the peace offering of the Lord is bright, as long as we look in the right direction and see through the cloudiness of past sorrows. As Elder Jeffrey R. Holland states, "He knows the way because He is the way" ("Broken Things to Mend," 71). The arms of grace can always dismantle uncertainties that we have in any circumstance we face. It's been said that a close relationship with the Lord can be like a lighthouse shining through the darkness. We consider ourselves lucky and blessed. Had life been led by chance, we would not have found each other. It was not by chance.

Just Between Us

Jen

I feel like Justin and I fell in love easily. We've always had incredible compatibility, and we love to be with each other. We knew that with work and dedication, we could steer through the obstacles that would stand in the way of not only getting married but of staying married, happily. Throughout our first years together, we have come to know each other on deeper levels. We've definitely both been pushed to our limits of patience and acceptance of the challenges that blending families brings. As we've grown closer, we've developed an understanding of each other's strengths and weaknesses. Our relationship is stronger because of it. We have progressed together in ways that we couldn't have progressed without each other. In getting married, we promised to be true to each other. We also took on commitments to raise our own kids and to raise each other's kids, equitably. Our children have needs specific to them.

Their needs arise often because of the difficult situations that none of them asked for. I'm grateful to have a husband that I can call my best friend; a husband that understands me. One who leaves messes for me to pick up. One who keeps me awake by snoring unless I fall asleep before he does. One who I can care for when he's struggling with mental illness. One who is learning that by helping our children with small things, he is providing comfort in ways that only a father can. One who likes to go on weekend getaways alone so that our relationship can be refreshed. One who I can rely on. One who always reminds me that I am loved.

Justin

Since the evening that Jen and I started communicating, we have continued to communicate without missing a day. It's strange to think about. I was living my life as a widower of eighteen months, unaware of the person that I would soon meet and marry. Suddenly she came into my life, and it has made all the difference. We feel like we've seen the best of each other and quite possibly the worst of each other. We've had plenty of hard moments. Moments of difficulty and moments of disagreement. We'll always face hard things, but if we are working together, things are never made harder. And we always know that when the storms come, there will be better days ahead for us.

Jen often worries herself in feeling that she's not being a good enough mother to our seven children, but she's mistaken in those worries. She is a great mother and a great wife. Many times we feel like we've landed on the other side of loss, and we always feel at peace together when we allow it to enter our hearts. That's not to say that pain is no longer there. The pain subsides, yet it will never go away. But when the strength to keep moving comes from the heart, we know that we can make it through the struggles.

Mountains in Front of Us

After more than three years of living in South Jordan, I'm still in awe at the view of the Wasatch mountains on the east side of the valley. They are majestic and magnificent. Mountains can teach us things. They are firm as they rise from the crust of the earth in strength and stability. Many mountains have beautiful peaks, with glaciers that withstand the summer heat without melting. Mountains cause us to look skyward.

Reaching the top of any mountain is an accomplishment. Mountain climbers often take gear to help them get past the crags and wedges of rock that lack the surface necessary to comfortably place their hands and feet in order to brace themselves and continue climbing upward. In most climbing postures, the force of gravity pulls in the opposite direction that the climber is reaching toward.

Mountains are often used to describe trials in our lives. These trials are the adversities that we face every day in which we must be strong and firm in our commitment to ourselves and to the Lord. Some of our largest mountains loom ahead of us, and regardless of our skills and expertise, we are not equipped with the ability to climb them on our own.

Despite our spiritual training, we require help. But they are our mountains, and we're not alone in facing them if we seek the safety net of the Lord's spirit to guide us. It's been said, "He rarely moves the mountains that stand in front of us, but He always helps us climb them" (Dew, "Sweet Above All That Is Sweet," *BYU Magazine*, fall 2014). If we expect the Lord to move our mountains for us, we can expect to be waiting for a long, long time—maybe even for the rest of our lives. When we rely on his ability to help us reach the top of the peaks and traverse to the other side of the mountains where great blessings reside, we can see the benefit of where we are and where we've been.

Blending families can feel like we're climbing mountains together—each one of us with unique trials. None of us could climb these mountains alone. Ever.

I've imagined all nine of us being at the peak of one of those mountains, seeing the hard work and blessings that got us there, and then realizing that there are much larger mountains called the Rockies beyond them.

As a family, we don't know what the challenges are that lie beyond the mountains that are currently in front of us. We struggle to reach each peak, but when we do, we share the thrill of looking back at how far we've come. And that's what inspires us to continue moving forward, knowing that we're there for each other and that the Lord is there to help us each as we climb.

A Brief Reflection

Anyone who stops to consider things realizes that life is filled with important moments. Some of them are hard, and some of them are easy. Some of them are easily noticed, while some of them take great effort to see and understand. If we step back and observe our lives sometimes, we can see important moments that take on meanings that we didn't know were there. In the words of Arthur James Russell, "Life with [God] is not immunity from difficulties, but peace in difficulties" (*God Calling* [1989]). I believe this is true. Our story of remarriage and blending families is not the story of any other family. It's unique to us. And the path is different for every member of our family.

In general, every Widow's and Widower's circumstances are their own story, and there is encouragement in knowing that God's plan for us will continue to unfold in his timing. Just remember that He hasn't forgotten you. He hasn't forgotten your family. Things might not have turned out as expected in life, but when we look back at our lives has anything ever turned out to be exactly as expected? We can still have confidence in the realization that God knows what's best for us and our families—past, present, and future.

References

Arthur James Russell. *God Calling: A Devotional Classic.* Dodd Mead, 1976.

Brown, Barbara Jones. "Growing as a Stepfamily." *Ensign*, July 2005.

Campbell, Kersten. "Widows and Widowers: Moving Forward with Faith." *Ensign*, January 2010.

Cordon, Bonnie H. "Becoming a Shepherd." *Ensign*, November 2018, 76.

Dew, Sheri. "Sweet Above All That Is Sweet." *BYU Magazine*, fall 2014, https://magazine.byu.edu/article/sheri-dew-sweet-above-all-that-is-sweet/.

Eliot, T. S. "Little Gidding." *The Complete Poems and Plays.* Harcourt, Brace & World, Inc., 1952.

Eyring, Henry B. "The Comforter." *Ensign*, May 2015, 20.

———. "Raise the Bar." Brigham Young University–Idaho Devotional. January 25, 2005, http://www2.byui.edu/Speeches/eyring_jan2005.htm.

Fisher, Rose-Lynn. *The Topography of Tears*. New York: Bellevue Literary Press, 2017.

Holland, Jeffrey R. "Broken Things to Mend." *Ensign*, May 2006.

———. "Created for Greater Things" Salt Lake City, Deseret Book, 2011.

———. "Like a Broken Vessel." *Ensign*, November 2013.

Kaur, Rupi. *The Sun and Her Flowers*. Kansas City: Andrews McMeel Publishing, 2017.

Lawrence, Larry R. "Daily Quote: Your Direction Is More Important Than Your Speed." Mormon Channel Blog. July 27, 2017, https://www.churchofjesuschrist.org/inspiration/latter-day-saints-channel/blog/post/your-direction-is-more-important-than-your-speed?.

Pace, Noelle Pikus. *Focused: Keeping Your Life on Track, One Choice at a Time*. Salt Lake City: Deseret Book, 2014.

Perry, Bruce D. *The Boy Who Was Raised as a Dog: And Other Stories from a Child Psychiatrist's Notebook*. Basic Books, 2007.

Robbins, Lynn G. "Daily Quote: Grow in Love." Mormon Channel Blog. February 9, 2017, https://www.churchofjesuschrist.org/inspiration/latter-day-saints-channel/blog/post/daily-quote-grow-in-love?lang=eng.

Rosenthal, Michele. *Your Life After Trauma: Powerful Practices to Reclaim Your Identity.* New York: W.W. Norton & Company, 2015.

Russell, A. J. *God Calling.* Uhrichsville, Ohio: Barbour Publishing, 1989.

Stephens, Carole M. "If Ye Love Me, Keep My Commandments." *Ensign,* November 2015.

Uchtdorf, Dieter F. "A Summer with Great-Aunt Rose," *Ensign,* November 2015.

———."'You Are My Hands.'" *Ensign,* May 2010, 70.

Web M.D. "Bipolar Disorder and Self-Injury." February 2018, https://www.webmd.com/bipolar-disorder/guide/bipolar-disorder-self-injury#1.

Wirthlin, Joseph B. "Come What May, and Love It." *Ensign,* November 2008.

Appendix

Widows' and Widowers' Closed-Forum Support Groups on Facebook

LDS Widows and Widowers
> The largest LDS private support group for the Widowed—5.4K+ members.

LDS Widows & Widowers Parent Awareness
> A private group where Widows and Widowers can exchange information about raising children.

LDS Widows & Widowers Tender Mercies Group
> A private support group for Widows and Widowers for dealing with complicated grief in recovering from difficult marriages and/or difficult circumstances.

Good Grief—The Lighter Side of Widowdom
> An LDS private support group that shares the funny and meaningful things that Widows and Widowers can appreciate—1K+ members.

LDS Young Widows & Widowers
A private support group for Widows and Widowers under 50.

Remarried Widows & Widowers—The Church of Jesus Christ of Latter-day Saints
An LDS private support group for remarried Widow & Widowers—400+ members.

LDS Blended Families
A private support group for Men and Women who are Blending Families.

LDS Widows & Widowers Events Group
A private support group that keeps its members informed about LDS Events and Conferences.

Latter-Day Saints Widows: Just Some Chick-Chat
A private support group for Widows to safely communicate privately about whatever is on their minds.

LDS Widowers (Men)
A private support group for Widowers who are not remarried.

LDS Remarried Widows
A private support group for Remarried Widows to share experiences in being Remarried.

LDS Remarried Widowers
A private support group for Remarried Widowers to share experiences in being Remarried.

LDS (Latter-Day Saints) Moms Blending Families Support

A private support group for LDS women to share stories and ideas about Blending Families.

Remarried Widows Retreats

A private support group that plans and carries out retreats for remarried Widows.

Please visit widowedandmovingforward.com to receive a download on ten things to consider before dating!

About the Authors

Justin T. Eller was born and raised in the Sacramento, California, area. He served in the Alabama Birmingham Mission for The Church of Jesus Christ of Latter-day Saints. He graduated from BYU–I with an associate's degree in 1995 and later received his bachelor's degree from the University of Utah in English. He did his graduate work in education at National University. Justin's late wife, Angela Sargent Eller, passed away in August of 2015 due to lung cancer. She is survived by Justin and their three children.

Jennifer M. Eller was born and has lived in the Salt Lake City, Utah, area her entire life. She graduated with an associate's degree in general studies from Salt Lake Community College in 1997. She has been blessed to be a stay-at-home mom for over twenty years. She has served over the youth and young women of The Church of Jesus Christ of Latter-day Saints for most of her adult life. She has participated in humanitarian efforts in Peru and Africa. Jennifer's late husband died by suicide in March of 2016. He is survived by Jennifer and their four children.

Justin and Jennifer were married on July 15, 2017. They currently reside in South Jordan, Utah.

Courtesy of jessicawhitephotography.com

CPSIA information can be obtained
at www.ICGtesting.com
Printed in the USA
LVHW020232150920
666028LV00001B/2